Essentials of Outcome Assessment

Essentials of Mental Health Practice Series

Founding Editors, Alan S. Kaufman and Nadeen L. Kaufman

Essentials of Interviewing
by Donald E. Wiger and Debra K. Huntley

Essentials of Outcome Assessment
by Benjamin M. Ogles, Michael J. Lambert, and Scott A. Fields

Essentials of Treatment Planning
by Mark E. Maruish

Essentials

of Outcome Assessment

Benjamin M. Ogles

Michael J. Lambert

Scott A. Fields

 John Wiley & Sons, Inc.

ISBN: 0-471-41998-2

Printed in the United States of America.

10   9   8   7   6   5   4   3   2

We would like to dedicate this book to the late Kenneth I. Howard, PhD, whose research and encouragement had a positive impact on us, the profession, and the many patients he strove to help.

CONTENTS

SERIES PREFACE

I n the *Essentials of Mental Health Practice* series, our goal is to provide readers with books that will deliver key practical information in an efficient
and accessible style. The series features books on a variety of critical
practice topics, such as interviewing, treatment planning, and outcomes assessment, to name a few. For the experienced professional, books in the series offer a concise yet thorough overview of a specific area of expertise,
including numerous tips for best practices. Students will find here a priori-
tized assembly of all the information and techniques that must be at one's
fingertips to practice knowledgably, efficiently, and ethically in today's behavioral health environment.

Wherever feasible, visual cues highlighting key points are utilized alongside systematic, step-by-step guidelines. Chapters are focused and succinct.
Topics are organized for an easy understanding of the essential material related to a particular practice area. Theory and research are continually wo-
ven into the fabric of each book, but always to enhance the practical application of the material, rather than sidetrack or overwhelm readers. With
this series, we aim to challenge and assist readers engaged in providing
mental health services to aspire to the highest level of proficiency in their
particular discipline by arming them with the tools they need for effective
practice.

In *Essentials of Outcome Assessment,* Ogles, Lambert, and Fields make practical recommendations regarding the implementation of outcome assessment in the typical clinical setting. The book is geared toward the practitioner who conducts outpatient psychotherapy. Many options for assessing

outcome are available, and this book surveys the broad variety of possibilities and quickly narrows in on the strategies and techniques thought to be the most useful for using outcome data in everyday work to monitor client progress. Global measures of change are reviewed along with suggestions regarding what changes to evaluate, when to gather, who to collect from, and how to assess outcome. Remaining chapters focus on the various other potential uses of the data such as developing the treatment plan, tracking progress for the individual client, evaluating therapists, enhancing clinical supervision, and supplementing program evaluation. Overall, the book provides practical, down-to-earth advice regarding the collection and use of outcome data in the outpatient practice of psychotherapy.

Alan S. Kaufman, PhD, and Nadeen L. Kaufman, EdD, Founding Editors
Yale University School of Medicine

One

OVERVIEW OF OUTCOME ASSESSMENT

Certainly the 1990s will be referred to in mental health service history as the decade of outcomes. In part because of tightened resources, the past few years have included increased responsibility or accountability for many types of health-related services. As a result of this focus, educational, medical, and mental health services in particular now are more closely scrutinized and managed using the collection of outcome data than at any time in recent history. The collection of outcome data is no longer limited to the randomized clinical trial or the researchers' lab. Data are routinely collected within agencies of all types to demonstrate the utility of services and to obtain consumer input regarding the quality and outcome of interventions provided. As a result, many clinicians and mental health service agencies are preparing to update their clinical practices through the implementation of outcome assessment strategies.

While psychological assessment issues are often highlighted in the psychological and counseling literature (e.g., Watkins, 1990), less has been written regarding the use of instruments for the assessment of outcome. It seems that researchers are often more interested in studying treatments than in examining the methods and measures used to demonstrate treatment effectiveness. However, to demonstrate that a treatment is beneficial, one must measure change. It is believed that clients should be different as a result of the therapeutic encounter, and these differences are meant to be beneficial for the client. As scientists, we also understand that our beliefs about patterns of client change and the associated effectiveness of our interventions are not enough. These changes must be measured and quantified in a manner that will let us make clear statements regarding the type and magnitude of change experienced by our clientele. In fact, Nunnaly (1978) has asserted that the central issue in social science research is measurement.

Standardized outcome measurement is not only a requirement of scientific rigor; the assessment of outcome is also an ethical obligation. Empirical evidence regarding the effects of our interventions, whether positive or negative, provides a basis for further understanding. When used with the individual client, standardized outcome assessment also generates quality assurance data that separate the professional from the charlatan or huckster. While the charlatan relies on selected case testimonials to justify using marginal treatments, the professional therapist understands the ethical obligation to provide objective evaluation of the quality of his or her services. To ensure continued faith in mental health treatment from the general public, mental health professionals need the support of objective data.

There is, however, another reason to be concerned with measuring outcome. Fiscal accountability is becoming a driving force behind the decisions of funding sources (e.g., third-party insurers, government agencies, and consumers), and mental health professionals will not escape their scrutiny. Monetary reimbursement will remain a viable option only for those who can demonstrate that their programs and practices are worthwhile (i.e., effective). Again, outcome assessment considerations are critical to demonstrating treatment utility. Rapid Reference 1.1 lists the primary purposes of outcome assessment.

In response to this increased focus on outcome assessment, several books (e.g., Clement, 1999; Cone, 2001; Hawkins, Mathews, & Hamdan, 1999; Lyons, Howard, O'Mahoney, & Lish, 1997; Maruish,

≡Rapid Reference 1.1

Reasons for Conducting Outcome Assessment

- to improve treatment
- to enhance clinical science
- to provide accountability
- to maintain the ethical responsibility of practitioners to examine quality

Barlow, Hayes, & Nelson, 1984; Ogles, Lambert, & Masters, 1996.

1999; Ogles, Lambert, & Masters, 1996; Sederer & Dickey, 1996; Speer, 1998) and articles (e.g., Bartlett & Cohen, 1993; Eisen & Dickey, 1996; Hodges & Wong, 1996; Kazdin, 1993; Koch, Lewis, & McCall, 1998; Lambert & Brown, 1996; Lambert, Ogles, & Masters, 1992; Ogles & Lunnen, 1996; Ogles, Lunnen, & Bonesteel, 2001; Weber, 1998) have been written in the past decade regarding the collection and uses of outcome data in practical settings. Similarly, state agencies, private boards, and others have established panels or task forces to make recommendations regarding the assessment of outcome (e.g., JCAHO, 1994; Vital Signs, 1998). Many providers are preparing to implement or are already implementing outcome collection strategies.

While becoming more responsible or accountable for services is a laudable goal, several difficult and complicating issues present problems for those who wish to engage in the practice of outcome assessment. This book introduces the essential elements of outcome assessment. We attempt to provide the key ingredients, tools, and instructions necessary to brew a tasty pot of outcome stew. Importantly, we also focus on using standardized instruments to provide individualized feedback. Use of standardized instruments allows the user to aggregate data for reporting purposes. At the same time, the main purpose of routine outcome assessment as described here is to track the progress of the individual client.

Before jumping into the practical details of outcome assessment, however, we provide a brief historical overview of the evolution of outcome assessment in research and practice (Chapter 1). Following this overview, we introduce the reader to several instruments that are used to assess outcome in outpatient behavioral health practice (Chapter 2). We then outline the basic procedural issues that must be addressed to engage in outcome assessment (Chapter 3). In the next three chapters, we describe the ways in which outcome assessment can inform clinical practice for the individual patient (Chapter 4) and for other purposes, such as program evaluation, marketing, or communicating with managed care (Chapter 5), including specific examples (Chapter 6). Finally, we draw some conclusions about the status of outcome assessment in clinical practice (Chapter 7). By succinctly distilling the central features of the outcome assessment process, we hope to give the reader the essentials of outcome assessment.

HISTORY OF OUTCOME ASSESSMENT

The earliest reports of therapy outcome were case studies in which the therapist reported the outcome of treatment without reference to any standardized assessment. In perhaps the first study of a group of patients, Fenichel (as cited in Bergin, 1971) reported on the outcome of individuals who received treatment at the Berlin Psychoanalytic Institute between 1920 and 1930. In this study, therapists (in this case psychoanalysts) rated clients as cured, very much improved, improved, uncured, still in progress, or prematurely terminated. Clients were not asked to provide any input regarding their view of the treatment outcome. Clients who did not complete treatment were not included in the final tally (prematurely terminated). Although the interpretation of the data was controversial (Eysenck, 1952), in the final analysis, 91% of the patients could be classified as improved (Bergin, 1971), lending early support to the efficacy of therapy.

From this humble beginning, psychotherapy research has gradually evolved into a significant scientific enterprise that involves thousands of publications per year in hundreds of journals. With such an overwhelming body of literature, finding general conclusions about the outcome of psychotherapy becomes increasingly difficult. Nevertheless, recent reviews (e.g., Lambert & Ogles, in press; Wampold, 2001) suggest several key findings when examining the literature at large.

Therapy is more effective than no treatment. When treatments are compared to no treatment in experimental conditions with clients randomly assigned to one of the two conditions, therapy produces quicker and larger benefits than no treatment. This finding has been substantiated through thousands of studies comparing treatments based on various theoretical orientations to no treatment and verified through hundreds of psychotherapy reviews. These reviews take two forms: (a) narrative reviews that describe the findings of a group of studies, and (b) meta-analytic reviews that quantify the findings of each study and summarize the results using a common metric or effect size; meta-analysis is defined in Rapid Reference 1.2. At the same time, there are many psychological interventions that have not been studied to date. In addition, these findings provide only a slight amount of useful information for the clinician regarding the next client who seeks service. "In this context, it is not sufficient for the practitioner to know that a particular treatment can work (efficacy) or does work (effectiveness) on average. . . . The practitioner needs to know what treatment is likely to work for a particular individual and then whether the selected treatment is working for this patient." (Howard, Moras, Brill, Martinovich, & Lutz, 1996, p. 1060). Practitioners desire data that can be helpful in specific situations with specific clients.

Therapy is more effective than a placebo treatment. Not only is therapy more effective than no treatment, but many psychotherapies have been compared to so-called placebo groups. In these studies clients are assigned to the treatment under study or to an experimental placebo group (i.e., a theoretically inert treatment discussed in more detail in Rapid Reference 1.3). Although there are numerous difficulties with the definitions of placebo groups, the therapy literature clearly illustrates that a bona fide treatment is indeed more effective than a placebo treatment. Again, however, studies of treatment in comparison to placebo provide little useful information for the clinician providing services to the next client who seeks service. One might conclude that the typical or average client is likely to benefit more from receiving a

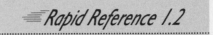

Rapid Reference 1.2

Definition of Meta-Analysis

Meta-analysis is a set of statistical procedures used to quantitatively examine and summarize the findings of multiple studies in a given area.

Rapid Reference 1.3

Placebos in Medicine and Psychology

In medicine, a *placebo* is an inert substance (such as a sugar pill) that is randomly given to a sample of participants and compared to the sample given the medical treatment in order to control for client expectations of success. Finding a true psychological placebo is much more difficult, however, and some might argue that all bona fide therapies include so-called placebo effects (e.g., expectations of success).

bona fide treatment than from receiving a psychological placebo (e.g., a nonspecific treatment that includes attention, expectations of success, warmth, etc.). However, many exceptions exist, and the research does not provide clues regarding the individual client sitting in the office at the moment.

Therapy can result in clinically meaningful improvement. For many clients seeking treatment, the benefits of participation are sufficiently large to be considered clinically meaningful. In an effort to better describe the benefits of treatment for the individual client, some researchers have identified methods for defining clinically meaningful improvement (cf. Ogles, Lunnen, & Bonesteel, 2001). They then use the methods to classify clients who have participated in studies of psychotherapy effectiveness into categories such as *clinically improved, reliably improved, unchanged,* and *deteriorated.* When examining the results of these studies, it is clear that many clients (perhaps as many as 40 to 50%) make reliable or clinically meaningful improvement depending on the type of problem being treated, the type of treatment being administered, and the method of categorizing clinical improvement (Ogles, Lunnen, & Bonesteel, 2001). Unfortunately, this also means that a rather large portion of clients do not make meaningful improvements. Approximately 5 to 10% of clients actually get worse during treatment, and the remaining clients make changes that are small enough to be considered no change.

Therapy results are often enduring. Importantly, the benefits of therapy are often enduring. Even when psychotherapists treat people with chronic problems such as addictions, many clients experience enduring relief from symptoms and show improved functioning over relatively long periods of time. Many studies include the assessment of client functioning at some point in time after treatment has ended. Although the duration of this follow-up is often brief (e.g., 3 to 12 months), most studies find that on average clients tend to maintain the gains that they achieved during treatment. This too is an important finding because if therapy were only effective on a short-term basis, then changes would need to be made so that the effects of therapy could last longer after treatment. The endurance of the positive effects of therapy continues to be a pivotal area of research for mental health professionals.

Research results may generalize to applied settings. One of the long-standing complaints of clinicians who attempt to make use of research findings is the frequent irrelevance of research to practice. Practitioners complain that therapy research is too focused on the average client and provides little information regarding the individual therapy consumer. In addition, treatments in research studies are often administered in a form that is quite different form therapy in the real world. For example, research protocols may limit participants to those with narrow diagnostic descriptions and may administer a standard length of treatment that is tightly controlled and closely monitored. In clinics, however, clients are treated for varying lengths of time based on many external factors such as the treatment model of the agency and the payment source. In addition, clients are not screened out if they have co-occurring diagnoses. As a result, some researchers and clinicians alike have asked whether therapy research can generalize to clinical practice. In studies that directly examine the effectiveness of therapy in applied settings combined with meta-analytic studies that evaluate whether effect sizes differ across various settings and levels of control (e.g., Wampold et al., 1997), the initial answer appears to be yes, therapy research does work in applied settings.

At the same time, the practice of therapy in most clinical settings substantially differs from treatment protocols administered in treatment studies. For example, the duration of therapy tends to be quite a bit shorter for the majority of clients seen in routine treatment when compared to a standard research treatment protocol (Hansen, Lambert, & Forman, in press). Similarly, *attrition,* or dropout in most clinical settings, defined in Rapid Reference 1.4, routinely hovers around 30 to 40% of clients following one or two sessions (Wierzbicki & Pekarik, 1993). As a result, the findings must be tempered by a lack of clear information regarding the benefit of treatment for these individuals who receive very small doses of treatment. Finally, these studies still ad-

≡*Rapid Reference 1.4*

Definition of Attrition

Attrition or dropout occurs when participants in studies do not finish the complete treatment protocol.

dress the issue of benefit for the average client and not for the individual client. Many individual clients remain unchanged or deteriorate in spite of the average benefit of treatment found in studies.

Summary and Criticisms

After many decades of intense scrutiny in rigorous clinical studies, the conclusions regarding the benefits of psychotherapy are appealing and satisfying for psychotherapy practitioners. There is solid evidence that therapy, on average, is efficacious and that its benefits exceed those of placebo treatments as well as no treatment at all. In addition, it is clear that many of the individuals who participate in psychotherapy receive clinically meaningful benefits that are maintained for lengthy periods of time following treatment and are not limited exclusively to the laboratory. This scientific evidence provides a firm foundation for the application of therapy in practice, and likely reassures therapists that what they are doing in practice is *generally* effective.

Unfortunately, therapy research provides relatively less useful information regarding the benefits of psychotherapy for the *individual* client. In addition, much of the therapy research is conducted in environments that differ from the typical clinic, using controls that alter the treatment sufficiently to raise doubts about the generaliz-

DON'T FORGET

Howard et al. (1996) list three fundamental questions in psychotherapy research.

1. Does the treatment work under special experimental conditions?
2. Does the treatment work in practice?
3. Is treatment working for this client?

The methods presented in this book are focused on the third question.

CAUTION

Although therapy research suggests that the *average* client will benefit from treatment, most therapy outcome research does not provide meaningful information that applies to the individual client who is currently receiving treatment.

ability of therapy research to practice. In short, therapy research is directed at two of the three fundamental questions that can be asked about any treatment (Howard, Moras, Brill, Martinovich, & Lutz, 1996): *Does the treatment work under special experimental conditions?* and *Does the treatment work in practice?* The third fundamental question, *Is treatment working for this client?,* is not directly addressed by the majority of psychotherapy and mental health service studies and reviews. This book and other recent articles and books address this fundamental weakness of the psychotherapy research literature. Indeed, it is the primary focus of this book to apply methods developed within psychotherapy research to answer this important question: Is treatment working for this client? (See Rapid Reference 1.5.)

Rapid Reference 1.5

Efficacy versus Effectiveness

Efficacy studies are conducted in the most ideal experimental conditions with carefully controlled treatments, random assignment, and selected patients and therapists. *Effectiveness* studies examine treatments in applied settings in which therapists and patients are assigned to treatment following normal clinical procedures and treatments are delivered as usual.

EVOLUTION OF OUTCOME MEASUREMENT IN RESEARCH

One important subtheme of the therapy research literature involves the gradual evolution of the instruments used as dependent variables (outcome measures) within the studies of therapy effectiveness. Although measurement and quantification are central properties of science, the earliest attempts at quantifying therapy gains lacked scientific rigor. Table 1.1 suggests several dimensions upon which assessments have varied since the focus of initial research on outcome assessment to the present. Whereas early studies relied primarily on the therapist as the source of outcome information, more recent studies include multiple viewpoints on therapy outcome. Similarly, early studies relied on global ratings of improvement or psychologically abstract and theoretically consistent measures of change (e.g.,

Table 1.1 Evolution of Outcome Measurement in Psychotherapy Research

Then	Now	Future
Therapist rated change	Multiple sources	Most important sources
Ratings of global change	Specific change/multiple technologies	Clinically significant changes
Bound to theoretical orientation	Practically important/ symptomatic	Practical and theoretical within disorder
Change is unidirectional	For better or worse	Predicting better and worse
Change is unidimensional	Change is multidimensional	Most important dimensions
Changes are stable	Changes are unstable	Predicting patterns

Source: Reprinted from Lambert, Ogles, & Masters (1992), page 528. Copyright ACA. Reprinted with permission. No further reproduction authorized without written permission of the American Counseling Association.

Thematic Apperception Test, Rorschach). Modern studies focus on more specific treatment effects using more clearly defined and atheoretical measures (e.g., symptom checklists). Early studies also focused only on improvement without considering the possibility that some clients may get worse. Similarly, early studies tended to focus on posttreatment outcome without following clients to assess the long-term outcome of treatment. Both of these weaknesses are more likely to be addressed in modern studies. In short, the field has gradually moved from a reliance on global therapist ratings of improvement to the use of more specific, multidimensional outcome instruments that are quantified from a variety of viewpoints, including those of the patient, outside observers, therapists, family members, and so on.

Although outcome measurement within therapy research has improved, many problems remain. For example, Meier and Davis (1990) documented one aspect of the assessment problem in outcome research. They reviewed the psychometric properties of outcome measures used in studies published in the *Journal of Counseling Psychology* for the years 1967, 1977, and 1987. Although recent investigators were more likely to use multiple measures within each study, approximately one third of the scales were either investigator-developed or -modified, and the modal number of items per scale was one! Clearly, the use of investigator-developed, one-item scales is not in the interest of science or practice.

Related to the problem of one-item, researcher-invented scales is the problem of divergence in measurement criteria. Although there is substantial agreement that multiple measures are an improvement over single measures (Gelso, 1979; Lambert, Christensen, & DeJulio, 1983; Oliver & Spokane, 1988), it appears that at present there are no consistent guidelines for the choice of instruments. For example, Froyd, Lambert, and Froyd (1996) reviewed assessment practices in outcome studies published in 20 major journals between the years of 1983 and 1988 and found no less than 1,430 distinct measures applied in 348 studies. The type, number, and quality of measures varied greatly across journals, disorders, and treatment methods. Further, Ogles, Lambert, Weight, and Payne (1990) found that great diversity exists even with homogeneous samples and treatments. They studied the assessment practices used in controlled outcome studies of agoraphobia published between 1980 and 1990. Nearly 100 ($N = 98$) separate measures were employed in the 106 studies analyzed. This is amazing diversity when one considers that the focus of treatment (agoraphobia), goals of treatment, and the interventions (mostly cognitive-behavioral therapy) were limited in scope. Similarly, Wells, Hawkins, and Catalano (1988) in their review of outcome studies of drug usage found 25 different procedures and measures that were used to assess drug use! Clearly, the scope of measures for outcome assessment is very broad.

The picture becomes even more clouded when we consider that in any given study, different measures of the same construct often fail to correlate. For example, Miller and Berman's (1983) meta-analysis suggested that treatment effects vary as a function of the source of measurement (e.g., client, therapist, other), and therefore the conclusions drawn about treatment effects may depend on whether the outcome data comes from one source rather than another. This diversity in measurement practices and results has made it difficult to sum across studies and draw sound conclusions about the effectiveness of specific treatments, interactions between treatment and client variables, and similar crucial issues. These questions can never be answered by a single-outcome study. The simplicity and lack of precision in early studies has given way to such great diversity and even chaos that there is an obvious need for integration and organization. And if this disorder exists within the research arena, how can the clinician make sense of the multitude of potential measures and methods when implementing outcome assessment strategies in practice? With literally thousands of measures used in research publications, how should the clinician select an appropriate measure?

Several research groups have attempted to bring a sense of order to the measurement of therapy outcome within psychotherapy research; some of these efforts cross over into the realm of applied evaluation. Waskow and Parloff (1975) organized a conference involving expert therapy researchers in an attempt to develop a core battery of instruments that could be used in all psychotherapy outcome studies. They suggested that in order to compare and integrate findings from different studies, a common set of instruments needed to be identified that could be used by researchers of various orientations. Despite these efforts, the past 25 years of measurement chaos document the conference's result. Strupp and Hadley (1977) proposed a tripartite model of mental health outcomes. They suggested that the three interested parties concerned with therapy outcomes were society, the client, and the mental health professional. Based on the viewpoint of the interested party, different criteria are selected to measure successful treatment. Lambert (1983) suggested that separate core batteries could be developed for specific disorders. Thus, agoraphobia researchers could use a standard battery of instruments that differed from the instruments selected by depression or drug treatment researchers. Gelso (1979) suggested eight dichotomous dimensions upon which outcome criteria vary. Cross, McDonald, and Lyons (1997) divide child mental health measures into eight categories: symptoms, behavioral problems, life functioning, family environment and behavior, self-esteem, measures for young children, client satisfaction, and other quality of care. They go on to describe six principles that might guide selection of measures depending on the needs of the organization along with describing several existing measures. Lambert, Ogles, and Masters (1992) describe a broad conceptual model for categorizing outcome measures. They discuss four characteristics of measures: the content, the source, the methodology or technology of data collection, and the time frame of each instrument. They also present a method for examining and selecting measures using the conceptual model. McGlynn (1996) identifies six primary outcome domains: clinical status, functional status, quality of life, adverse events, satisfaction with care, and expenditures. Finally, Rosenblatt and Attkisson (1993) outline a conceptual framework for outcomes related to services for individuals with severe mental disorders. Their three-dimensional model includes the domain of outcome assessment, the respondent, and the social context of the assessment. The domain of outcome assessment can include one of four areas of treatment outcome: clinical status, functional status, life satisfaction and fulfillment, and safety and health.

In perhaps the most comprehensive effort to date, Ciarlo et al. (1986) summarized a set of guidelines for the development, selection, or use of outcome measures. These guidelines were developed by a panel of experts who were assembled via National Institute of Mental Health (NIMH) funding (see Newman, Ciarlo, & Carpenter, 1999). The guidelines present a mix of instrument characteristics including five categories: application of the measures (e.g., relevance to the target group), methods and procedures (e.g., simple methods), psychometric features (e.g., reliability), cost, and utility considerations (useful, easy feedback). The guidelines are then used to examine the various features of a variety of outcome instruments. The inclusion of methods, utility, and cost within this system make it unique in its perspective regarding the assessment of outcome. While many instruments are developed for the assessment of outcome in treatment research, the selection criteria are often limited to the psychometric characteristics of the instruments. As a result, some instruments may not be easily transferred to the applied setting. Because this system includes an evaluation of practical and psychometric characteristics, it is relevant to both the researcher and the clinician seeking to assess outcome.

Interestingly, problems with outcome measures were also evident in the

1970s (Bloom & Fischer, 1982). For example, Ihlevich and Gleser (1982) summarize their work on the Progress Evaluation Scales (PES) after discussing the problems that agencies encountered when attempting to evaluate mental health services. Among the difficulties mentioned in their book, they suggest that "standardized instruments for measuring outcome that are reliable, valid, and relevant for clinical and programmatic decision making yet are sufficiently broad to be applicable to the great variety of programs and clients served by mental-health professionals in the community are largely unavailable" (Ihlevich & Gleser, 1982, pp. 1–2). This problem continues to exist in the 21st century, but it need not loom larger.

As can be seen, a number of valiant efforts have attempted to bring increased order to the selection of outcome instruments in counseling and psychotherapy *research* (e.g., Strupp, Horowitz, & Lambert, 1997). In addition, several specific efforts (e.g., Newman, Ciarlo, & Carpenter, 1999; Ogles, Lambert, & Masters, 1996) focused on developing conceptual or organizational methods for clinicians to use when selecting instruments for evaluation of practice. (More is said about how to use these principles when selecting among measures in the next chapter.) In spite of these efforts both in the research arena and in practice, the proliferation of outcome measures and methods makes it extraordinarily difficult for the clinician who is attempting to begin a systematic process of evaluating outcome within his or her practice. At the same time, the psychotherapy research has produced findings sufficiently useful to allow some practical applications of measures and methods. As we continue in the following chapters, we hope to provide high-quality advice regarding the selection of measures, the routine use of measures in practice, and the application of both individual and group outcome data.

THE APPLICATION OF THERAPY RESEARCH METHODS IN PRACTICE

Although the findings of therapy studies may not provide information for the current client sitting in a therapist's office, the methods developed by the therapy researcher may still be utilized to benefit the client. And although the proliferation of outcome measures may seem chaotic, several useful research-based measures are available for ready application in clinical settings. More specifically, the following list identifies some of the potential contributions of therapy outcome research that may be used by the clinician in the assessment of outcome.

1. The general findings of the psychotherapy research literature provide a foundation of confidence for the benefits of psychotherapy and suggest that the average client will improve when receiving a bona fide psychological treatment.

2. A select group of measures developed for the study of psychotherapy may often be useful for the clinician. Although a large number of measures are developed and used once (Froyd, Lambert, & Froyd, 1996), some measures have been subjected to rigorous evaluation and are used in both experimental and applied settings with a great deal of success. These measures may be used by the clinician to assess the effectiveness of treatment for the individual client.

3. Statistical techniques developed by researchers may also be applied in practice. While most clinicians do not have the resources to enter and analyze data for each individual client, analytical methods can be instantaneously and routinely employed using current technology so that feedback regarding client progress can be quickly provided to the therapist with little effort. For example, with relative ease client progress could be mechanically examined using expected and actual growth curves followed by generating reports for the clinician. Although the statistical modeling could be quite complicated, the therapist need not completely understand the calculations so long as the fundamental principles of the technique are understood and the reports are usable.

4. Even without fancy technology, simple feedback regarding client progress using standardized outcome measures can be readily infused into existing information systems. Indeed, some measures

are sufficiently practical so that the therapist could complete the calculations and comparisons in a few minutes.

5. Finally, the growing body of so-called patient-oriented literature provides some of the fundamental data necessary for comparative purposes. That is, client expected improvement is typically calculated based on the aggregate data from other similar individuals. Without a normative sample or comparison group, the expected rates of improvement cannot be estimated. Research can provide data that establish models for expected improvement, deterioration, and so on.

Although this does not provide an exhaustive list of the contributions of research to practice, it clearly illustrates that some portions of the therapy research are ready-made for application to current practice. In short, by using measures developed by researchers, clinicians can administer the measures repeatedly over time to track client progress. In addition, statistical procedures fine-tuned in the laboratory along with aggregate data gathered in research studies or clinical databases can provide relatively simple methods for identifying clients who are not progressing as expected. In this way, the clinician can obtain feedback regarding the client's current progress and the degree to which it deviates from that which is expected. In addition, aggregate data can also be used to describe the effects of a treatment, a program, a therapist, or an agency.

One example may help to illustrate that the methods used in a psychotherapy study might be readily applied to practice. Lambert, Whipple, Smart, et al. (2001) found that they could identify potential treatment failures based upon the patient's initial level of disturbance and early negative response to treatment. Therapists were given feedback in the form of a colored marker and written message. Green and white markers indicated the patient was responding as expected, or that the patient had entered the ranks of normally functioning individuals (based on normative samples on the symptom measure). Red and yellow markers were given for patients whose progress was negative, along with a message that instructed therapists to review the case, consider alterations in the treatment plan, or initiate discussions with the patient about his or her worsening condition.

In this study, 10% of patients were identified as alarm signal cases (not progressing as expected). Providing feedback to therapists about patients' conditions enhanced outcomes and reduced deterioration (compared to a randomly assigned control group) for alarm signal cases. Those patients identified as potential treatment failures whose therapists received feedback also remained in therapy longer than no-feedback controls identified as potential treatment failures. A replication of this study (Lambert, Whipple, Vermeersch, et al., in press) resulted in essentially the same findings, reinforcing the notion that patient deterioration can be reduced if therapists are alerted to the possibility early in treatment. This and related quality improvement methods aimed at reducing deterioration are not yet widely employed by managed care or by practitioners. However, the methods are sufficiently elementary so that an individual clinician or several clinicians in a group practice could easily develop a system for tracking client change and identifying alarm signal cases. Indeed, we shall illustrate some of the procedures in later chapters.

SUMMARY

In this chapter we briefly covered some of the major findings of the psychotherapy outcome literature and reviewed the evolution of outcome measurement within therapy research. Although the research literature builds the confidence of the therapy practitioner, the findings provide relatively little information that can be applied for the individual client. Similarly, the large number of outcome measures used in research provides a bewildering array of options for the clinician who is interested in implementing outcome assessment in practice. At the same time, some measures and methods available in the therapy research, especially those from within a new breed of patient-oriented studies, provide useful methods that can be readily applied in practice. In the remaining chapters the measures and methods of outcome assessment are described in sufficient detail to allow the practitioner to select and implement a routine outcome data collection system in practice.

🖋 TEST YOURSELF 🖋

1. **Studies on the clinical significance of psychotherapy have found that psychotherapy patients, after treatment, exhibit *clinically significant* changes**

   (a) about half the time.

   (b) most of the time.

   (c) all of the time.

   (d) less than a quarter of the time.

   (e) only if given medication.

2. **Which of the following statements is most representative of the overall findings of the psychotherapy literature?**

   (a) Psychotherapy is efficacious.

   (b) Psychotherapy is more beneficial than placebo treatment.

   (c) Psychotherapy effects are relatively enduring.

   (d) Psychotherapy produces clinically significant results for many clients.

   (e) All of the above.

3. **The central issue in social science research is**

   (a) investigation of length of time in therapy.

   (b) pharmacotherapy.

   (c) measurement.

   (d) client satisfaction with services.

   (e) finding representative samples.

4. **Which of the following are reasons to conduct outcome assessment?**

   (a) Improvement of treatment

   (b) Enhancement of clinical science

   (c) Provision of accountability

   (d) Ethical responsibility of practitioners to examine quality of services

   (e) All of the above

5. **The typical attrition or dropout rate in psychotherapy after one or two sessions is about**

   (a) 30 to 40%.

   (b) 10 to 15%.

   (c) 70 to 80%.

   (d) Less than 5%.

   (e) None of the above.

6. **Which of the following is true of the evolution of outcome measures in psychotherapy research?**

   (a) Early studies assessed outcome at the end of treatment and follow-up.

   (b) Recent studies usually assess only one dimension or construct of change.

   (c) Recent studies do not look for clients who deteriorate during treatment.

   (d) Recent studies often include multiple sources of outcome.

   (e) All of the above.

7. **Based on recent studies, which of the following is a problem with outcome measurement today?**

   (a) There is a paucity of outcome measures.

   (b) Existing outcome measures are overly standardized.

   (c) Too much divergence exists in measurement criteria.

   (d) Clients feel burdened by the completion of outcome measurements.

   (e) Government funding of outcome assessment is not available.

8. **Client expected improvement can be calculated based on the aggregate data from other similar individuals. This typifies the clinical utility of**

   (a) laboratory settings.

   (b) patient-oriented data.

   (c) textbooks.

   (d) clinic-oriented data.

   (e) circumscribed data.

Answers: 1. a; 2. e; 3. c; 4. e; 5. a; 6. d; 7. c; 8. b.

Two

SELECTING AN OUTCOME MEASURE

Perhaps the most important part of instituting an outcome assessment process in a program, practice, or agency is the selection of the outcome measure(s). An efficient, well-run organization that routinely attempts to assess outcome will have meaningless data if the measurement instrument is poor. Surprisingly, many agencies and clinicians develop their own outcome measures to gather input from consumers regarding services received. Often these measures are limited to brief satisfaction questionnaires. These surveys, however, may be unreliable or invalid and interfere with accurate interpretation of the information. In addition, satisfaction is one view of outcome, but it provides little in the way of pertinent information regarding client change. As a result, most agencies would do better to incorporate research-based measures into their clinical routines in order to gather outcome data with better reliability and validity.

At the same time, many research-based instruments are lengthy, costly, or difficult to score and interpret. In fact, the demands placed on instruments used for outcome assessment are often unrealistic. For example, when asked about the characteristics that would make a useful outcome measure, practitioners often hope that the instrument can serve multiple purposes. It would be nice to have an instrument that can screen for serious issues at intake (e.g., self-harm, drug or alcohol abuse), provide information regarding a broad range of potential problems (diagnostic symptoms), and provide pretreatment data for later comparison with posttreatment data (outcome). At the same time, users require that the instruments be short, easy to understand, easily scored, inexpensive, and psychometrically rigorous. These demands create natural tensions that evolve from the multiple competing desired uses and characteristics of outcome. Indeed, one could argue that an outcome measure cannot incorporate all uses and characteristics at the same time. As a result, careful selection of a measure is imperative, and the selection should be based on the most important uses and characteristics as defined by the user.

Within this chapter, we present the preparatory steps that are necessary before choosing measures; we also offer tips for selecting among measures based on the tensions that evolve from the competing uses and characteristics.

PREPARATION

Before selecting a measure, the clinician must take several preparatory steps. For example, Cross, McDonald, and Lyons (1997) in the context of children's mental health services summarize the preliminary steps to outcome assessment in the following way:

> Because of issues of cost, time and the state of the art in instrument development, outcome measurement in children's mental health does not always answer the need for information. There is no standard set of outcome measures that is appropriate for every program in every situation. It is therefore important to consider two fundamental issues around the goals and design of an evaluation. 1) What questions most need to be addressed? and 2) What measures are appropriate to address these questions? (p. v)

This chapter addresses these two questions and provides descriptions of some of the most practical measures that are available for immediate use. Before describing and selecting the measures, however, one must focus on the appropriate questions. To determine which questions to address, Cross, McDonald, and Lyons (1997) describe six principles that might guide selection of measures depending on the needs of the organization along with describing several existing measures: "1) Start with program goals, 2) Consider the level of development of the program, 3) Involve stakeholders, 4)

Assess resource need and availability, 5) Identify sources of information, and 6) Consider the nature of the population" (p. 2).

Through an examination of these issues the clinician can be better informed regarding the needed end product. For example, an outcome system developed with the goal of gathering aggregate data for marketing purposes may differ significantly from an outcome system developed to monitor individual client progress as feedback to the therapist. The outcome system that is developed in an attempt to handle both of those goals will need an outcome measure that can balance between the two needs. Because there are many pros and cons among the various uses of outcome measures, it is important to have a clear understanding of the purpose for the outcome assessment in the first place. Returning now to the six principles of Cross et al., we would like to note that the typical outpatient service can be reasonably represented. In Table 2.1, the application of the six principles to the usual outpatient service is described. As can be seen, we are assuming that the primary reader is a therapist, supervisor, or administrator within an agency or practice that provides outpatient behavioral health services—therapy. We are also assuming that the primary goals or purposes of implementing the outcome assessment process can be approximated in the following list.

1. To assess the progress of each individual client receiving treatment
2. To make decisions regarding ongoing treatment based on data regarding the direction of the client's progress (e.g., no change, deterioration, improvement)
3. To enhance supervision through direct evidence of client progress via outcome measurement
4. To have data available to inform the payor (e.g., managed-care case managers) regarding the progress of clients whose treatments are funded by their institutions
5. To aggregate data across clients in order to produce reports that may be useful for internal evaluation and administration (e.g., therapist effectiveness, program effectiveness, investigation of

Table 2.1 Application of Cross et al.'s (1997) Six Principles to the Typical Outpatient Provider

Principle	Typical Outpatient Therapy Application
Start with program goals.	The goal is to provide effective, high-quality outpatient therapy.
Consider the level of development of the program.	Even when new, outpatient treatment programs have similar administration and rapid development.
Involve stakeholders.	Both clients and therapists contributed to the development of many existing outcome measures. Involvement of clients in the development of an outcome system may also be helpful.
Assess resource need and availability.	Time and cost are almost always at a premium for outpatient providers. As a result, inexpensive, practical measures are highly desirable.
Identify sources of information.	The primary sources are client (or parent) and therapist.
Consider the nature of the population.	Outpatient behavioral health population: Some characteristics may vary and require differing measures or implementation to match outcomes to the population.

  differences among clients from various diagnostic groups or referral sources)
6. To create reports for external consumption (e.g., marketing, contracting)

Given these assumptions about outpatient practice and the purpose of outcome assessment, we take some liberties by narrowing the questions and measures that we discuss in the remaining portions of the book. For example, several other books regarding outcome assessment (Clement, 1999; Hawkins, Mathews, & Hamdan, 1999; Ogles, Lambert, & Masters, 1996; Wiger & Solberg, 2001) emphasize or include major sections on an individualized approach to outcome measurement. These individualized approaches evolve from the long history of behavioral research and treatment, which naturally included self-monitoring, case studies, and other tailored, individual approaches to the identification of target behaviors to track (and modify) during treatment. Although this type of outcome assessment has many positive and important qualities, we prefer using standardized instruments for several reasons (e.g., strong psychometric properties of the standardized instruments, potential for meaningful aggregation of data). As a result, a description of individualized outcome measurement approaches is provided later in this chapter, but our focus remains largely on standardized instruments.

Although we have narrowed the focus and goals based on our assumptions regarding the needs of most clinicians in practice, a large number of instruments are available for assessing outcome. As a result, we now present a model for selecting among measures along with making specific recommendations (based on the original assumptions) regarding who, what, and when to measure outcome as well as how to use outcome data in practice. In essence we consider the following questions: What content areas or domains of outcome should be measured? Who should provide the data? When should the data be collected? And how should the data be collected and reported? Each of these questions will be discussed while we consider natural tensions that exist within the world of outcome assessment that influence what, who, when, and how to measure outcome. Finally, selected outcome measures are described.

A GUIDING MODEL FOR THE SELECTION OF A MEASURE

In order to help guide the process for selecting among outcome measures, several authors have developed categorical or conceptual models of outcome measurement. In a previous book (Ogles et al., 1996), we described a broad conceptual model for categorizing outcome measures that includes five characteristics of outcome measures: the content, the social level, the source, the methodology or technology of data collection, and the time frame of each instrument (see Table 2.2).

The content of the measure is the psychological construct that is being

Table 2.2 Organizational and Conceptual Scheme for Categorizing Outcome Measures

Content	Social Level	Source	Technology	Time Orientation
Cognition	Intrapersonal	Self	Global	Trait
1	1	1	1	1
2	2	2	2	2
o	o	o	o	o
Affect	Interpersonal	Therapist	Specific	State
1	1	1	1	1
2	2	2	2	2
o	o	o	o	o
Behavior	Social Role	Trained Observer	Observation	
1	1	1	1	
2	2	2	2	
o	o	o	o	
		Relevant Other	Status	
		1	1	
		2	2	
		o	o	
		Institutional		
		1		
		2		
		o		

Source: From Ogles, Lambert, & Masters, *Assessing Outcome in Clinical Practice.* Copyright 1996. Reprinted by permission by Allyn & Bacon.

assessed such as depression, anxiety, or interpersonal difficulties. Measures may address rather broad content areas such as severity of symptoms (e.g., the Symptom Checklist-90-Revised; SCL-90-R) or more narrowly defined symptoms (e.g., the Fear Questionnaire). In general, three broad categories of contents are often the focus of outcome measures: change in cognition, affect, or behavior. At the same time, most instruments include items that cover all three potential content categories. Thus, all three content areas are typically addressed in most outcome measures used.

The social level category refers to the social focus of the instrument (e.g., intrapersonal, interpersonal, or social role). Outcome measures may target individual change, the change that occurs within dyads or other interpersonal relationships, or more broad social functioning (e.g., work). An evaluation of a patient's social functioning is often key in determining how well that person is responding to treatment.

The source of the instrument refers to the person providing the information (e.g., client, therapist, trained judge, family member). The client or therapist will generally be the main source of outcome data in applied settings because of the practical demands of such settings. This issue is discussed later in this text in greater detail.

The technology or methodology of the instrument is the prescribed method used to gather the data; it also coincides with typical effect sizes when using a given instrument (e.g., global, specific, status). Some outcome measures focus on more global change whereas others focus on change in specific, narrowly defined or targeted behaviors or symptoms. Other measures of change in the research literature include observational measures (e.g., behavioral approach tests in the treatment of phobias) or measures of status (e.g., recidivism, hospital discharge, heart rate).

Finally, the time frame refers to the interval that is suggested for use of the instrument. Some instruments are used only following treatment, whereas others are recommended for pre- and post-treatment assessment. Others may be used at more frequent intervals, and some are available for use at every session or service event.

By examining various measures according to these categories, the clinician can gain much comparative information regarding selected instruments. When matching the specific needs of the outcome system with certain dimensions, the clinician can begin to select a measure that matches his or her needs. For example, to select a measure for an adolescent with disruptive behavior, the clinician can first determine the content area that is preferred (in this case, disruptive behaviors); the clinician may also prefer to have the parent ratings as the primary source. Similarly, the clinician would like to have information about both intrapersonal and interpersonal change in the adolescent client. If the clinician decides to gather data before and during treatment, the instrument must be one that is sufficiently brief to be used frequently. Given the preferences on these four dimensions, the various measures that are available can be gathered

> **CAUTION**
>
> No single outcome measure will be useful for every clinician or agency. A variety of factors (such as cost, utility, program goals, resources, etc.) will influence the selection of a measure.

and examined as to the various methodologies. In short, all parent-rated, disruptive behavior instruments that include items regarding both intrapersonal and interpersonal functioning of the adolescent can be gathered, provided the selected instruments are brief enough to be administered repeatedly. Some of these instruments may focus on more global change whereas others may be specific to certain types of disruptive behaviors (e.g., Attention-Deficit/Hyperactivity Disorder, oppositional behaviors). Some may be daily observations of disruptive behaviors, whereas others may be rating scales. The clinician can then select from among these measures based on his or her needs and preferences. In addition to offering this conceptual model as a way of comparing measures, we offer three guiding, overarching principles to consider when selecting among measures.

Principle I—Know the Trade-Offs

Clinicians or organizations that are selecting among outcome assessment devices will value different content areas. Some facilities are most interested in behavioral change, while others may be interested in cognitive change. A clinic focused on family therapy will be more interested in interpersonal change than would be a group of psychotherapists who prefer information regarding intrapersonal change. Facilities providing services to individuals with chronic disturbances may desire assessment devices that evaluate changes in social role performance (e.g., vocational status, living

DON'T FORGET

Three key principles can guide the selection of an outcome measure.
1. Know the trade-offs among the measures.
2. Know the audience for your outcome data.
3. Recognize the resource (time and cost) limitations.

arrangements). Selecting measures in this way is largely a matter of preference. At the same time, every measure has distinct advantages and disadvantages. Knowing the pros and cons of each decision will help the organization to make informed decisions about the trade-offs among the potential solutions. As we further discuss the various questions and measures, we will illustrate the pros and cons of each choice in order to help the clinician make an informed decision.

Principle 2—Know Your Audience

When deciding who, what, and how to measure, it is important to know who your ultimate audience will be. Private corporations receiving Employment Assistance Program (EAP) services will not be impressed if the therapists complete all of the outcome data. The employers want to know that their employee-consumers are satisfied and improving. Select measures based on who will get the final information. We suspect that most therapy practitioners generally have multiple audiences, including at a minimum the therapist, the client/consumer, the administrator, and the payor. As a result, the selection of an outcome measure and system of data collection will necessitate balancing the needs of each of these audience members.

Principle 3—Recognize Resource Limitations

Adding outcome assessment to routine clinical business can be expensive and time consuming. Knowing the potential consequences of adding two measures versus one measure will help the clinician to make a sound decision. The challenge is selecting inexpensive, practical, and brief measures that still meet the quality demands of the organization. In addition, it is important to consider the impact of additional paperwork when adding outcome assessment at various intervals (e.g., pre-post, every session, etc.).

CAUTION

Every instrument has some negative features. No method of collecting outcome data is without problems. As a result, it is important to acknowledge the limitations of your instrument and of your assessment process whenever you report the findings of your outcome evaluation.

A myriad of potential measures and methods have been developed for the ongoing assessment of client change. As a result, the costs and benefits of obtaining outcome information from different sources using a variety of methodologies must be considered before selecting the most practical instruments. Even after careful thought, however, each method has its own specific strengths and weaknesses, which must be acknowledged when producing reports for aggregated data or examining the individual client's progress.

The primary focus of this book is the use of outcome assessment data for the clinician to guide the treatment process for each individual client. It is true that these same data can be aggregated and used for other purposes (e.g., program evaluation, marketing) and we give examples of these uses, too. However, the primary use of outcome assessment, as we are describing it, is tracking change for the individual client and providing feedback to the clinician regarding the client's progress. Naturally, this focus will strongly influence what we measure and who provides the information. The next two sections of this chapter focus on two specific questions: What to measure? and Who provides the outcome information?

WHAT TO MEASURE?

The natural tensions that accompany every decision regarding the selection of a measure and development of a procedure for collecting outcome data strongly influence the decision concerning what to measure. A variety of potential outcome systems are available with more or less sophistication.

Every scenario may include different content areas of outcome assessment. Should the clinician select a global measure of symptoms that can be used for a large majority of the clients? Or should the clinician select several different measures that can be used for clients with various presenting problems or diagnoses? Should the clinician develop different outcome assessment strategies for different programs within a given agency or use a uniform outcome assessment measure and method for the entire organization? These questions are not just a matter of preference, but also come with distinct disadvantages and advantages. We present here the pros and cons of several different content areas along with our recommendation.

Three primary content areas should be considered for use in the typical outpatient setting: (a) a global measure that is appropriate for the large majority of clients receiving services, (b) multiple specific measures that are used for certain programs or populations, and (c) individualized outcome assessment. In addition, a brief excursion into the satisfaction content area deserves our attention.

Global Measures of Outcome

Perhaps the most practical method of assessing therapy outcome, and our recommended strategy for most clinicians and agencies providing outpatient services, is to select one global measure of change that can be used for all clients seeking services. For example, the Brief Symptom Inventory (BSI; Derogatis & Melisaratos, 1983) provides an index of current distress related to a mix of undesirable symptoms including anxiety, depression, and so forth. The majority of clients attending outpatient treatment will endorse a number of symptoms on the BSI and when compared to clinical samples will likely be identified as someone with a clinical level of distress. As a result, the client could then be administered the instrument multiple times during treatment to track progress or at the end of treatment to investigate the amount of improvement.

Global measures of outcome have several advantages, but the biggest advantage is that they can be used with all clients who receive services. Routines for administering and interpreting the measures can be easily developed and need not vary as would be necessary if the agency were to administer different instruments to certain clients. Global measures typically provide an index of overall severity of distress that can be compared to a normative sample. Global measures are also easier to aggregate, facilitating uniform reporting. Finally, global measures provide direct, meaningful information to the clinician regarding the client's current level of distress or functioning.

Several global measures of outcome are available for use in applied settings. We selected six instruments for description here: the Symptom Checklist–90–Revised (SCL-90-R®), the Brief Symptom Inventory (BSI®), the Outcome Questionnaire (OQ-45®), the Behavior and Symptom Identification Scale (BASIS-32), the Short Form–36 Health Survey (SF-36®), and the Clinical Outcomes in Routine Evaluation (CORE) system.

The Symptom Checklist–90–Revised (SCL-90-R)
The SCL-90-R (Derogatis, 1983) is a 90-item measure that requires approximately 12 to 15 minutes for the client to complete. Hand scoring requires approximately 15 to 30 additional minutes (if scoring all scales). The items are rated on a 5-point scale of distress (0 = not at all; 1 = a little bit; 2 = moderately; 3 = quite a bit; 4 = extremely). There are nine primary symptom dimensions (somatization, obsessive-compulsive, interpersonal sensitivity, depression, anxiety, hostility, phobic anxiety, paranoid ideation, psychoticism) and three global indexes of distress (global severity index, positive symptom distress index, and positive symptom total index), of which the most important is the Global Severity Index (GSI). The GSI is the best single indicator of the current level of distress. The GSI is based on all 90 items and is often used as a single global measure of outcome because it combines information on the number of symptoms and the intensity of the perceived distress. The use of a computer for scoring and reporting on this measure is also available.

Reliability estimates for the SCL-90-R are acceptable. Internal consistency coefficients ranged from .77 for Psychoticism to .90 for Depression (Derogatis, 1994). Test-retest coefficients are also strong, ranging from .78 for Hostility to .90 for Phobic Anxiety over a 1-week interval, and .68 for

Somatization to .83 for Paranoid Ideation over a 10-week interval (Derogatis, 1994). For validity, the internal structure was reportedly found to match well with the hypothesized factor structure on most of the primary symptom dimensions (Derogatis, 1994). The results of convergent-discriminant validity tests displayed strong correlations with the MMPI on all of the symptom dimensions except Obsessive-Compulsive (Derogatis, 1994). The SCL-90-R has also been shown to be very sensitive to levels of distress in a wide range of settings ranging from measurement of change to sexual dysfunction (Derogatis, 1994). For example, the SCL-90-R displayed a treatment effect of .82 in brief dynamic psychotherapy (Derogatis, 1994).

The SCL-90-R was one of the original instruments recommended by Waskow and Parloff (1975) as a measure that should be included in a core battery of instruments for assessing the outcome of psychotherapy in research. It has also received some use in clinical settings, although it is much less prominent there than in research programs (Piotrowski & Keller, 1989). Rapid Reference 2.1 provides some additional information about the SCL-90-R, including ordering and scoring information.

Brief Symptom Inventory (BSI)

The Brief Symptom Inventory (Derogatis & Melisaratos, 1983) is a brief version of the SCL-90-R that reflects the same nine symptom dimensions and three global indexes but has fewer (53) items. As a result, the administration and scoring time is slightly quicker. Computer scoring and reporting on this measure are also available, thus further streamlining the process; Rapid Reference 2.2 provides some additional information about the BSI.

Reliability estimates show strong internal consistency and test-retest reliability. The internal consistency coefficients for the nine primary symptom dimensions ranged from .71 for Psychoticism to .85 for Depression (Derogatis, 1993). Test-retest coefficients for all the subscales over a 2-week period ranged from .68 for Somatization to .91 for Phobic Anxiety (Derogatis, 1993). Convergent validity is also high between the BSI symptom dimensions and the MMPI (17 correlations with coefficients ≥ .30)

≡ Rapid Reference 2.1

Symptom Checklist–90–Revised (SCL-90-R)

Number of items—90

Forms—self-report

Approximate administration time—15 minutes

Scales/Scores—12

- Somatization (12 items)
- Obsessive-Compulsive (10 items)
- Interpersonal Sensitivity (9 items)
- Depression (13 items)
- Anxiety (10 items)
- Hostility (6 items)
- Phobic Anxiety (7 items)
- Paranoid Ideation (6 items)
- Psychoticism (10 items)
- Global Severity Index (average of all 90 items)
- Positive Symptom Distress Index (average of nonzero responses)
- Positive Symptom Total (number of nonzero responses)

Availability—The SCL-90-R is available through National Computer Systems (NCS) at 1-800-627-7271, ext. 5151 or through the Internet at http://assessments.ncs.com/assessments/tests/scl90r.htm.

Cost—Hand scoring starter kits can be purchased for approximately $2 per test including manuals, templates, and so on, and replenished for somewhat less.

Computer scoring—Computer scoring is available through NCS for a per-use fee that depends upon the type of report (e.g., interpretive versus profile) and method (mail-in versus home personal computer program).

and very high correlations (coefficients range from .92 to .99) exist between the BSI and the SCL-90-R (Derogatis, 1993). The predictive validity of this measure has been shown to be quite strong in a variety of settings ranging from screening to therapeutic interventions (Derogatis, 1993). As with the SCL-90-R, the Global Severity Index is the best single measure of

Rapid Reference 2.2

Brief Symptom Inventory (BSI)

Number of items—53

Forms—self-report

Approximate administration time—5 to 10 minutes

Scales/scores—11

- Somatization (7 items)
- Obsessive-Compulsive (6 items)
- Interpersonal Sensitivity (4 items)
- Depression (6 items)
- Hostility (5 items)
- Phobic Anxiety (5 items)
- Paranoid Ideation (5 items)
- Psychoticism (5 items)
- Global Severity Index (average of the 53 items)
- Positive Symptom Total (number of nonzero responses)
- Positive Symptom Distress Index (average of nonzero responses)

Availability—The BSI is available through National Computer Systems (NCS) at 1-800-627-7271, ext. 5151 or through the Internet at http:// assessments.ncs.com/assessments/tests/bsi.htm.

Cost—Hand scoring kits can be purchased for approximately $2 per test including manuals, templates, and so on, and replenished for somewhat less.

Computer scoring—Computer scoring is available through NCS for a per-use fee that depends upon the type of report (e.g., interpretive versus profile) and method (mail-in versus home personal computer program).

distress and the most frequently used measure of progress when examined repeatedly over time.

The Outcome Questionnaire (OQ-45)

The OQ-45 (Lambert, Hansen, Umphress, et al., 1996; Lambert, Burlingame, Umphress, et al. 1996) is a 45-item self-report measure that uses a 5-point scale. Each item is rated using a 5-point scale (0 = never, 1 = rarely, 2 = sometimes, 3 = frequently, 4 = almost always), and several items are reverse scored. Three subscales are included: symptom distress, interpersonal relations, and social role functioning. The three areas of functioning are measured to cover a continuum of content areas from how the person feels inside, how he or she is getting along with significant others, and how he or she is doing in important life tasks (e.g., work and school). The measure usually takes about 5 minutes to administer. Rapid Reference 2.3 provides some additional information about the OQ-45.

For reliability, internal consistency tests showed that the item total and the symptom distress subscale had a coefficient above .90, whereas the other two subscales ranged between .70 and .74 (Lambert & Finch, 1999).

≡Rapid Reference 2.3

Outcome Questionnaire (OQ-45)

Number of items—45

Forms—Self-report

Approximate administration time—5 minutes

Scales/Scores—4

- Total (Total of all 45 items)
- Symptom Distress (25 items)
- Interpersonal Relationships (11 items)
- Social Role Performance (9 items)

Availability—Paper-and-pencil versions of the OQ-45 are available through American Professional Credentialing Services LLC at P.O. Box 477, Wharton, NJ 07885-0477 or through the Internet at http://www.oqfamily.com/.

Cost—Use of the paper-and-pencil version of the OQ-45 requires a one-time licensing fee that varies depending on the size of the organization. Computer scoring rights are available for a per-use fee.

Computer scoring—Computer scoring is available through OQ Systems at http://www.oqsystems.com/.

Test-retest reliability showed coefficients that ranged from .86 to .66 over a 7-day period (Lambert & Finch, 1999). Concurrent validity estimates indicated that the OQ-45 total and scale scores are correlated with the Inventory of Interpersonal Problems ($r = .66$ to .81; Horowitz et al., 1988) and the SCL-90-R ($r = .78$ to .88; Derogatis, 1983; Lambert & Finch, 1999). For construct validity, the measure was found to discriminate between inpatient and community populations. In addition, the sensitivity for the OQ-45 was .84 and the specificity .83 (Lambert & Finch, 1999). Additional evidence of validity is presented in the test manual and other articles (e.g., Mueller, Lambert, and Burlingame, 1998; Umphress, Lambert, Smart, Barlow, & Clouse, 1997; Vermeersch, Lambert, & Burlingame, 2000).

The OQ-45 was specifically created to measure patient progress in therapy—the total score is most frequently used as the indicator of change. The OQ-45 was also designed to be practical (brief, inexpensive) yet psychometrically rigorous (reliable, valid, sensitive to change). Items were selected to assess commonly occurring problems across a wide variety of disorders and to address the symptoms most likely to occur in clients seeking outpatient treatment. The OQ-45 is self-administered and requires no instructions beyond those printed on the instrument itself.

Scoring the OQ-45 involves summing the client's ratings across all 45 items (range 0 to 180). The Symptom Distress, Interpersonal Relations, and Social Role scores are calculated by summing the client's ratings on 25, 11, and 9 items, respectively. Templates to facilitate scoring have been designed and a computer scoring service is available including interactive voice technology, web administration, and so forth.

Behavior and Symptoms Identification Scale (BASIS-32)
The BASIS-32 (Eisen, Grob, & Klein, 1986; Eisen, Dill, & Grob, 1994; Eisen & Culhane, 1999) is a 32-item self-report measure developed to assess mental health status and assess outcome for clients receiving psychiatric care. The BASIS-32 uses a 5-point scale (0 = no difficulty, 1 = a little difficulty, 2 = moderate difficulty, 3 = quite a bit of difficulty, and 4 = extreme difficulty). Client responses are averaged to create a total score and five subscale scores: Relation to Self/Others, Depression/Anxiety, Daily Living/Role Function-

ing, Impulsive/Addictive Behavior, and Psychosis. Rapid Reference 2.4 provides some additional information about the BASIS-32.

Test-retest reliability for the subscales over the period of a week varied from .65 for Impulsive/Addictive behavior to .81 for Daily Living/Role Functioning. The overall test-retest reliability for the total score was .85 (Eisen, Dill, & Grob, 1994). The internal consistency coefficient for all items was .95, and subscales ranged from .65 for Impulsive/Addictive Behavior to .89 for Relation to Self/Others (Eisen & Culhane, 1999). Construct validity estimates between the BASIS-32 and the SF-36 demonstrated very strong correlations for the subscales Relation to Self/Others, Depression/Anxiety,

≡Rapid Reference 2.4

Behavior and Symptom Identification Scale (BASIS-32)

Number of items—32

Forms—self-report (can also be administered as a structured interview)

Approximate administration time—5 to 10 minutes

Scales/Scores—6

- Overall average (Average of the 32 items)
- Relation to Self/Others (7 items)
- Daily Living/Role Functioning (7 items)
- Depression/Anxiety (6 items)
- Impulsive/Addictive Behavior (6 items)
- Psychosis (4 items)

Availability—Permission to use the BASIS-32 may be obtained by contacting the Department of Mental Health Services Research at McLean Hospital, 115 Mill Street, Belmont, MA 02478-9106 or through the Internet at http://www.basis-32.org/.

Cost—An annual site license can be purchased to use the BASIS-32 at the address above.

Computer scoring—The BASIS-32 Plus Performance Measurement System is available at the aforementioned address. This expanded system meets JCAHO reporting requirements.

and Daily Living/role functioning, with somewhat weaker correlations for Impulsive/Addictive Behavior and Psychosis (Eisen & Culhane, 1999). The measure was also shown to be sensitive to client changes between intake and follow-up tests (Eisen & Culhane, 1999). For discriminant validity, the BASIS-32 was able to discriminate between inpatient and outpatient populations. In addition, the subscale Depression/Anxiety was able to discriminate clients with depression or anxiety, however, the Impulsive/Addictive behavior and Psychosis subscales failed to discriminate significantly among respective groups of clients (Eisen & Culhane, 1999).

Short Form–36 Health Survey (SF-36)

The SF-36 (Ware, 1999; Ware, Snow, Kosinski, & Gandek, 1993) is a 36-item measure that uses a five-choice response scale and requires 5 to 10 minutes for the client to complete. Within the measure are eight subscales (Physical Functioning, Role-Physical, Bodily Pain, General Health, Vitality, Social Functioning, Role-Emotional, and Mental Health) and two summary measures (Physical Component and Mental Component). Both hand scoring and computer scoring are available; more information about the SF-36 is available in Rapid Reference 2.5.

The SF-36 has displayed strong reliability over many tests. Most reliability statistics have exceeded .80, while the two summary measures usually exceed .90 (Ware, 1999). Tests also show the eight subscales have median reliability coefficients of .93 (Ware, 1999). Validity tests have shown that the content validity of the SF-36 is comparable to that of other generic health surveys. Eight of the most commonly represented health concepts are also found in the SF-36 (Ware, 1999). The most valid mental health measures among the subscales are the Mental Health, Role-Emotional, Social Functioning, and the Mental Component summary measure (Ware, 1999). Of the physical health measures, Physical Functioning, Role-Physical, Bodily Pain, and the Physical Component summary measure have been shown to be the most valid (Ware, 1999). In addition, the Mental Health subscale and the Mental Component summary measure are both effective in screening for psychiatric disorders. Tests on predictive validity have linked the SF-36 and the summary measures to the clinical course of

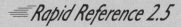

Short Form–36 Health Survey (SF-36)

Number of items—36

Forms—self-report

Approximate administration time—5 to 10 minutes

Scales/Scores—6

- Overall average (Average of the 32 items)
- Relation to Self/Others (7 items)
- Daily Living/Role Functioning (7 items)
- Depression/Anxiety (6 items)
- Impulsive/Addictive Behavior (6 items)
- Psychosis (4 items)

Availability—Permission to use the SF-36 may be obtained by contacting QualityMetric, Inc., 640 George Washington Highway, Lincoln, RI 02865 or http://www.sf-36.com.

Cost—Single user, noncommercial royalty-free licenses may be obtained at the address above. Multiuser noncommercial groups and commercial users must pay a royalty fee that is based on the number of SF-36 administrations per year.

Computer scoring—Scoring services are available through Qualitymetric at the aforementioned address.

depression and loss of job within 1 year (Ware, 1999). Factor analysis tests have also shown that the Physical Function, Role-Physical, and Bodily Pain are often the most responsive to the benefits of certain surgeries such as hip replacements and heart valve surgery (Ware, 1999). The Mental Health, Role-Emotional, and Social Functioning, however, tend to be more responsive to changes such as the severity of depression and the use of drug treatment and interpersonal therapy for depression (Ware, 1999).

Clinical Outcomes in Routine Evaluation (CORE-OM) System

The CORE-OM (Barkham et al., 1998) is a client self-report measure that was developed to assess the central features of client change. The 34-item measure is also available as two 17-item short forms (a and b). The items are rated on a 5-point scale—0 (not at all) to 4 (most of the time). The instrument was developed after a thorough review of the literature, a survey of practitioners and other therapy stakeholders, and a consideration of practical issues (Barkham, Margison, Leach et al., 2001). Rapid Reference 2.6 provides more information about the CORE-OM.

The reliability and validity of the CORE-OM are satisfactory. The internal consistency of all 34 items is excellent (alpha = .94) and the subscales range from .77 to .90. Similarly, test-retest reliability was satisfactory with reliability estimates ranging from .64 to .88 for the subscales and .90 for the average of all items. The scale discriminates clinical from nonclinical samples and is correlated with other measures of distress (e.g., Beck De-

≋Rapid Reference 2.6

Clinical Outcomes in Routine Evaluation (CORE-OM)

Number of items—34

Forms—self-report

Approximate administration time—5 to 10 minutes

Scales/Scores—5

- Overall average (Average of the 34 items)
- Subjective Well-Being (4 items)
- Symptoms (12 items)
- Functioning (12 items)
- Risk/Harm (6 items)

Availability—Forms for hand or computer scoring can be obtained by contacting the CORE system group in Leeds, England, telephone 0113 233 1984/1988/1990 or fax 0113 233 1956.

Cost—If scored by hand the measure is free of charge (so long as the measure is not changed and no profit is gained through its use).

Computer scoring—Computer scoring can be accomplished through sending the forms to the CORE system group for processing.

pression Inventory, Brief Symptom Inventory, Inventory of Interpersonal Problems). Overall, the CORE-OM is an excellent, practical measure of outcome.

In addition to these global measures of outcome for adults, we present three global measures of outcome for children. The assessment of outcome within children's behavioral health services can be especially challenging. Because the development of outcome assessment tools for children's behavioral health services lags behind the efforts for adults (Weber, 1998), there is a paucity of quality measures. Nevertheless, we present three useful measures here: the Ohio Youth Problems, Functioning, and Satisfaction Scales (Ohio Scales), the Child Behavior Checklist (CBCL), and the Youth Outcome Questionnaire (Y-OQ®).

The Ohio Youth Problems, Functioning, and Satisfaction Scales (Ohio Scales)

The Ohio Scales (Ogles, Melendez, Davis, & Lunnen, 2001) were developed with the hope of making a unique contribution to the evaluation of mental health services for youth by combining several important instrument characteristics: practicality, multiple content areas, multiple sources, and psychometric rigor. The final goal was a set of instruments that would emphasize the practical characteristics that are useful for agencies and practitioners (e.g., brief, easy scoring; easy interpretation; reasonable price) while maintaining psychometric rigor. In addition, multiple constructs were included in one brief measure (in parallel form for multiple raters) rather than relying on the use of a battery consisting of multiple independently produced measures. Rapid Reference 2.7 provides some additional information about the Ohio Scales.

The Ohio Scales have adequate internal consistency (alphas range from .72 to .95 in both clinical and community samples) and test-retest reliability (range from .67 to .88). Similarly, validity has been established through correlations with other similar established measures such as the CBCL and Youth Self Report YSR ($r = .89$ and $r = .82$, respectively) and the ability to discriminate between clinical and nonclinical samples (Ogles, Melendez, Davis, & Lunnen, 2001).

≡Rapid Reference 2.7

Ohio Youth Problems, Functioning, and Satisfaction Scales (Ohio Scales)

Number of items—44

Forms—Parent, youth, agency worker

Approximate administration time—5 to 10 minutes per form

Scales/Scores—4

• Problem Severity (20 items)

• Functioning (20 items)

• Satisfaction with services (4 items)

• Hopefulness (4 items)

Availability—Permission to use the Ohio Scales may be obtained by contacting the Southern Consortium for Children, P.O. Box 956, Athens, OH 45701-0956 or through the Internet at http://oak.cats.ohiou.edu/ogles.

Cost—A one-time licensing fee that varies depending on the size of the organization allows unlimited copying and use of the Ohio Scales.

Computer scoring—The Ohio Scales are available through various vendors for telephone entry, scannable forms, digital entry, etc. (see aforementioned web address). Licensed users may also develop their own computerized scoring programs.

The Child Behavior Checklist (CBCL)

The CBCL (Achenbach, 1991; Achenbach & Edelbrock, 1983) is a parent- or parent surrogate–rated measure of child problem behaviors and competencies. The problem scales consist of 112 items that are rated using a three-point scale (0 = not true, 1 = somewhat or sometime true, and 2 = very true or often true). Eight syndrome subscales are included in the measure: Withdrawn, Somatic Complaints, Anxious/Depressed, Social Problems, Thought Problems, Attention Problems, Delinquent Behavior, and Aggressive Behavior. A ninth subscale, Sex Problems, is included in the tests for ages 4 to 11. In addition to the syndrome subscales, three competence scales are measured with an additional set of items (20 items): Activities, Social, and School. To reflect sex and age differences, there are six dif-

Child Behavior Checklist (CBCL)

Number of items—118 (Problem Scale), 15 (Social Competencies)

Forms—parent, teacher, direct observation, youth self-report

Approximate administration time—20 to 30 minutes

Scales/Scores—15

- Total (116 items)
- Internalizing (sum of Withdrawn, Somatic, and Anxious)
- Externalizing (sum of Delinquent and Aggressive)
- Withdrawn (9 items)
- Somatic Complaints (10 items)
- Anxious/Depressed (14 items)
- Social Problems (8 items)
- Thought Problems (7 items)
- Attention Problems (11 items)
- Delinquent Behavior (13 items)
- Aggressive Behavior (20 items)
- Activities (5 items)
- Social (6 items)
- School (4 items)
- Total Competence (sum of 3 competence scales)

Availability—The CBCL and associated instruments can be ordered from University Associates in Psychiatry at 1 South Prospect Street, Burlington, VT 05401-3456 or through the Internet at http://www.aseba.org/index.html.

Cost—The CBCL is available for purchase at a per-form fee (50 forms for $25 not including scoring templates, manuals, etc.).

Computer scoring—a variety of software products are available for the CBCL and associated instruments at the above address.

ferent editions of the profile, one for each of the different groups. The group divisions are as follows: boys age 4 and 5, boys age 6 to 11, boys age 12 to 16, girls age 4 and 5, girls age 6 to 11, and girls age 12 to 16. The procedure of comparing individual profiles to group profiles can be done either by hand or with the assistance of a computer. In addition, the CBCL can be supplemented by a host of other forms of the instrument for youth self-report, direct observation, structured interview, teacher report, or younger children. However, the parent-rated CBCL is the version that is most commonly used to assess outcome both in practice and in child outcome research. More information about the CBCL is provided in Rapid Reference 2.8.

For test-retest reliability, the mean coefficient for all of the scales over a 7- to 15-day period was .88 (Achenbach, 1999). Interparent agreement is also adequate, ranging from .54 to .87. Construct validity tests showed that the CBCL can discriminate between referred and nonreferred children (Achenbach, 1999). In addition, the measure is significantly correlated with other similar scales (Achenbach, 1999).

Youth Outcome Questionnaire (Y-OQ)

The Y-OQ (Burlingame, Wells, & Lambert, 1996) is a measure that the parent completes using a 4-point scale (0 to 4) and usually requires only 5 to 10 minutes to administer. In addition to the total sum of the items, six subscales are included in the Y-OQ: Intrapersonal Distress, Somatic, Interpersonal Relations, Social Problems, Behavioral Dysfunction, and Critical Items. Additional information about the Y-OQ is provided in Rapid Reference 2.9.

Internal consistency coefficients for the scales ranged from .76 for Somatic and Critical items to .93 for Intrapersonal Distress (Wells, Burlingame, & Lambert, 1999). The internal consistency for the total score was .97 (Wells, Burlingame, & Lambert, 1999). Test-retest reliability at a 2-week interval, .84, and 4-week interval, .81, was acceptable (Wells, Burlingame, & Lambert). The Y-OQ and the CBCL are significantly correlated, $r = .78$, while tests for construct validity showed that this measure was able to discriminate between clinical and nonclinical populations (Wells, Burlingame, & Lambert, 1999). In addition, the sensitivity of the

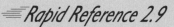

Rapid Reference 2.9

Youth Outcome Questionnaire (Y-OQ)

Number of items—45

Forms—self-report

Approximate administration time—10 minutes

Scales/Scores—7

- Total (Total of all 45 items)
- Intrapersonal Distress
- Somatic
- Interpersonal Relations
- Social Problems
- Behavioral Dysfunction
- Critical Items (9 items)

Availability—Paper-and-pencil versions of the Y-OQ are available through American Professional Credentialing Services LLC at P.O. Box 477, Wharton, NJ 07885-0477 or through the Internet at http://www.oqfamily.com/.

Cost—Use of the paper-and-pencil version of the Y-OQ requires a one-time licensing fee that varies depending on the size of the organization. Computer scoring rights are available for a per-use fee.

Computer scoring—Computer scoring is available through OQ Systems at http://www.oqsystems.com/.

measure was found to be .77 and the specificity .81 (Wells, Burlingame, & Lambert, 1999).

Although the practical advantages of using a global measure are numerous, using global measures also presents some disadvantages. Global measures may not include items or content that is relevant and necessary to assess change for some clients who are seeking services. For example, the Ohio Scales has no items that are specific to encopresis. As a result, parents seeking service for their child regarding encopresis may rate their child as having few problems because the appropriate content is not available on the instrument. At the same time, the child may be exhibiting concurrent disruptive and oppositional behaviors or experiencing emotional distress (e.g., depression, anxiety) along with the central problem—the encopresis. In that case, the global measure may still be sensitive to co-occurring change in secondary behaviors. Global measures are also not as relevant to the individualized format of treatment planning. Although individual items can be examined and incorporated into the treatment planning, the central, client-identified problems that bring clients to treatment may not be represented on the instrument. Finally, when global measures are used repetitively during treatment to track progress, the items that are not relevant may become aversive to the client because such items are repeatedly asked and contain material that is not central to the client's treatment.

Although global measures have some disadvantages, their practical value makes them our recommended option. A set protocol for administering a global measure can be easily developed in a clinic. For example, one behavioral health provider asked clients to rate the Outcome Questionnaire at intake, the 3rd session, the 6th session, the 10th session, and every 10 sessions thereafter. All clients participated in this set protocol. This procedure seems more efficient than selecting from among multiple measures that may fit better with the clients' presenting problems. At the same time, the disadvantages of global measures (e.g., their potential for a poor fit with some clients) will result in some agencies' or clinicians' selecting a menu of more specific measures that are administered to clients based on matching client problems with measures.

Specific Measures of Outcome

A more sophisticated or client-specific method of administering outcome measures in a practice or agency would be to collect several measures that address the issues of the typical clients served. For example, a clinician who specializes in the treatment of chronic pain or eating disorders may be better served by instruments selected to assess outcome specifically with these populations. Especially for populations that have rather unusual symptoms that may be missed by more global symptom measures (e.g., substance abuse, enuresis), the use of specific measures may be necessary to assess outcome. At the same time, most psychological disorders include the presence of broad-based symptoms, distress, or impairment in functioning that is detected by global measures. Nevertheless, some clinicians or agencies may wish to assess outcome more specifically. For example, a clinician who has a general practice in outpatient therapy with mostly individuals who have symptoms of depression and anxiety may select two measures that are appropriate for assessing the outcome of these two general categories of clients. For clients with depression as the primary feature of their presentation, the clinician would administer the depression-oriented outcome measure during the intake and after treatment. For clients with anxiety as the primary feature of their presentation, the clinician administers the anxiety-focused instrument during the intake and after treatment. In this way, the outcome measures are more specific to the client's presentation and may be more relevant to treatment. The measures may also be more sensitive to change because the targets of treatment are more likely to be included in the outcome instrument. In addition, the use of just two specific measures maintains some of the advantages of the global measures (e.g., normative comparison samples are available, data can be aggregated for all clients taking the same measure).

Numerous specific instruments are available for assessing outcome with certain clients. The majority of these instruments were developed based on the research literature regarding interventions for individuals with certain diagnoses (e.g., depression, Agoraphobia, Obsessive-Compulsive Disorder, etc.). Indeed, research groups that conduct a series of studies that investigate the efficacy of a treatment for a given disorder often use a battery of outcome instruments repeatedly. For example, P. M. G. Emmelkamp has conducted numerous studies regarding the effectiveness of treatments for Agoraphobia (e.g., Emmelkamp, Kuipers, & Egerraat, 1978). In each of these studies a relatively consistent set of outcome measures was used. In fact, Ogles and Lambert (1989) conducted a meta-analysis of six studies that used the same 12 measures in order to compare the relative effect sizes of the measures. The measures of outcome were observer-rated client anxiety related to the main phobia, observer-rated client avoidance of main phobia, observer-rated client anxiety related to other phobias, observer-rated client avoidance of other phobias, client-rated anxiety related to the main phobia, client-rated avoidance of the main phobia, client-rated anxiety related to other phobias, client-rated avoidance of other phobias, the Fear Survey Schedule, the Internal-External Locus of Control, the Self-Rating Depression Scale, and time outside during an in vivo test (the client was instructed to go outside the clinic until he or she felt uncomfortable or tense). Clearly, a battery of such instruments is not appropriate for clinical use, but some of the measures might have clinical applications.

A few measures that are specific to certain populations are described here. These measures were included because they are appropriate for clients who are often treated within typical outpatient services (e.g., individuals with depression or anxiety disorders). A large number of other measures are available for these same content areas and other more specific groups of clients (e.g., individuals with eating disorders, chronic pain, substance abuse). A complete cataloging of the potential specific measures available for the assessment of outcome is beyond the scope of this book. For those clinicians who have more specialized practices, the principles described earlier may help to identify useful measures. Similarly, the principles and illustrations provided later in this text regarding the implementation of outcome assessment with global measures apply equally to using specific measures. Clinicians need only substitute the instrument that is appropriate for the group of individuals they serve within the assessment protocols that are described.

Beck Depression Inventory (BDI®)

The BDI (Beck, Ward, Mendelson, Mock, & Erbaugh, 1961) is a 21-item self-report measure that usually requires 10 to 15 minutes to administer and score. A 4-point scale (0 to 3) is used and 21 symptoms are measured: mood, pessimism, sense of failure, lack of satisfaction, guilt feelings, sense of punishment, self-dislike, self-accusation, suicidal wishes, crying, irritability, social withdrawal, indecisiveness, distortion of body image, work inhibition, sleep disturbances, fatigability, loss of appetite, weight loss, somatic preoccupation, and loss of libido. The BDI is the most frequently used outcome measure in psychotherapy studies with depressed clients

(Nietzel, Russel, Hemmings, & Gretter, 1987). The BDI is also used frequently in clinical practice (Piotrowski & Keller, 1989). Rapid Reference 2.10 provides some additional information about the BDI.

Internal consistency estimates from different populations all resulted in high coefficients (ranging from .73 to .95; Katz, Katz, & Shaw, 1999). Test-retest estimates of reliability found that nonpsychiatric patients (.60 to .83) showed more stability than psychiatric patients (.48 to .86) (Katz, Katz, & Shaw, 1999). Tests for content validity between the BDI and the *DSM-III* criteria for a depressive episode indicate that the BDI has good validity for six of the nine criteria. The BDI also correlates highly with other measures of depression (e.g., Zung Self-Reported Depression Scale, $r = .86$) and with a variety of clinician's ratings ($r = .96$; Katz, Katz, & Shaw, 1999). In addition, studies on discriminant validity find that the BDI is able to distinguish between depressed and nondepressed individuals (Katz, Katz, & Shaw, 1999); however, the BDI appears to be less successful in discriminating among depressive disorders (Beck, Steer, & Garbin, 1988). Overall, the BDI is a practical instrument for assessing depressive

≡Rapid Reference 2.10

Beck Depression Inventory (BDI)

Number of items—21

Forms—self-report

Approximate administration time—5 to 10 minutes

Scales/Scores—1

Total (Total of the 21 items)

Availability—The BDI and BDI-II can be obtained through the Psychological Corporation at 555 Academic Court, San Antonio, TX 78204-2498 (1-800-211-8378) or through the Internet at http://www.pscyhcorp.com.

Cost—The BDI and BDI-II are available on a per-form basis. Kits (including manuals) can be purchased at the aforementioned address.

Computer scoring—Computer scoring is available for the BDI-II through Psychological Corporation, but is not available for the original BDI.

symptoms; it has an impressive research history and adequate psychometric properties.

The State-Trait Anxiety Inventory (STAI)

The STAI (Spielberger, 1983; Spielberger, Gorsuch, & Lushene, 1970) is a self-report measure that provides a brief index of anxiety. This instrument is a frequently used outcome measure in studies of treatment for anxiety; more information about the STAI is provided in Rapid Reference 2.11. The test is divided into state anxiety (S-Anxiety) and trait anxiety (T-Anxiety) scales. The state anxiety scale is rated using a 4-point scale (1 = not at all, 2 = somewhat, 3 = moderately so, and 4 = very much so). The trait anxiety scale is rated using a similar format with different anchors (1 = almost never, 2 = sometimes, 3 = often, and 4 = almost always). Test-retest coefficients for the T-Anxiety scales were adequate for both college students (.73 to .86) and high school students (.65 to .75) whereas the S-Anxiety scale had a median coefficient of .33 (Spielberger, Sydeman, Owen, &

≡Rapid Reference 2.11

State-Trait Anxiety Inventory (STAI)

Number of items—40

Forms—self-report

Approximate administration time—10 minutes

Scales/Scores—2

• State anxiety (S-Anxiety; 20 items)

• Trait anxiety (T-Anxiety; 20 items)

Availability—The STAI is available through Multi-Health Systems Inc. (MHS) at 908 Niagara Falls Blvd., North Tonawanda, NY 14120-2060 or through the Internet at http://www.mhs.com.

Cost—The paper-and-pencil STAI can be purchased for approximately $1 per form; computerized scoring and interpretation are available for a per-report fee.

Computer scoring—Scoring programs can be purchased from MHS at a per-use fee (see aforementioned address).

Marsh, 1999). Because of the transient nature of state anxiety, test-retest correlations are not informative. For internal consistency, T-Anxiety scales had high alpha coefficients with a median of .90, and S-Anxiety scales had alpha coefficients with a median of .93 (Spielberger et al., 1999). For concurrent validity, the T-Anxiety scale had a high correlation with other measures of anxiety, ranging from .73 to .85 (Spielberger et al., 1999). Construct validity tests for T-Anxiety scale showed that it could discriminate between those with anxiety and those without; the S-Anxiety scale was able to discriminate between those in a stressful situation and those in a nonstressful situation (Spielberger et al., 1999). Of the two scales, the state scale seems to be the most useful. Among other advantages, it is sensitive to change and can be administered repetitively over short intervals.

Fear Questionnaire (FQ)

The Fear Questionnaire is the most frequently used standardized scale for measuring outcome in Agoraphobia treatment studies (Ogles et al., 1990). It was developed by Marks and Mathews (1978) to assess outcome from the client's perspective in phobia treatment studies. The FQ includes 24 items that are rated on a 9-point scale, from *Would not avoid it* to *Always avoid it*, or from *Hardly troublesome at all* to *Very severely troublesome*. In addition to a global phobia index, there are three subscales: Agoraphobia, Blood-Injury Phobia, and Social Phobia. Five additional items measure anxiety and depression that are associated with the client's phobia. The Agoraphobia subscale or the total phobia score are typically used as outcome measures in treatment studies. Additional information about the FQ is provided in Rapid Reference 2.12.

Test-retest reliability was shown to be strong for the main target phobia ($r = .93$), the global phobia rating ($r = .79$) and the anxiety and depression symptoms ($r = .82$) (Corcoran & Fischer, 1987). The Agoraphobia, Blood-Injury Phobia, and Social Phobia subscales combined displayed a test-retest coefficient of .82 for 1-week (Corcoran & Fischer, 1987). Validity tests indicate that the FQ is sensitive to change, and every aspect of the test is able to discriminate between phobic and nonphobic patients (Corcoran & Fischer, 1987). Mizes and Crawford (1986) report that the advantages of the Fear

Rapid Reference 2.12

Fear Questionnaire (FQ)

Number of items—24

Forms—self-report

Approximate administration time—5 to 10 minutes

Scales/Scores—5

- Total Phobia (15 items)
- Agoraphobia (5 items)
- Blood-Injury Phobia (5 items)
- Social Phobia (5 items)
- Anxiety and Depression (5 items)

Availability—The Fear Questionnaire is available through the original journal article or other publications (e.g., Corcoran & Fisher, 1987; Ogles, Lambert, & Masters, 1996).

Cost—free

Computer scoring—None is available.

Questionnaire include its brevity, its emphasis on common phobias, its inclusion of Agoraphobia, and its emphasis of Agoraphobia and Social Phobia items over simple phobia. Oei, Moylan, and Evans (1991) suggest that the Agoraphobia and Social Phobia subscales can help identify whether an individual has Agoraphobia or Social Phobia. They also report normative data for four diagnostic categories: Agoraphobia, Social Phobia, Generalized Anxiety Disorder, and Panic Disorder Without Agoraphobia. Normative data are also available in other publications (Mathews, Gelder, & Johnston, 1981; Mizes & Crawford, 1986; Nietzel & Trull, 1988; Trull, Nietzel, & Main, 1988). The Fear Questionnaire is widely used in research. It is a brief, practical measure that could be easily used in clinical settings.

Dyadic Adjustment Scale (DAS)

The Dyadic Adjustment Scale (Spanier, 1976) is a 32-item, self-report measure of relationship satisfaction in couples. The DAS is widely used in couples therapy research, and it is perhaps the instrument of choice in clinical settings. The DAS can be used either as a general measure of satisfaction in a relationship, or as a measure of satisfaction in four areas: dyadic satisfaction, dyadic cohesion, dyadic consensus, and affectional expression. Several studies, however, suggest that the DAS is composed of a single factor, a general measure of relationship satisfaction (Kazak, Jarmas, & Snitzer, 1988). Most of the 32 items use a 7-point scale ranging from *always agree* to *always disagree* or from *all the time* to *never*. Six items use a 5-point scale and one item has a 6-point scale. Rapid Reference 2.13 provides more information about the DAS.

≡Rapid Reference 2.13

Dyadic Adjustment Scale (DAS)

Number of items—32

Forms—couple-report

Approximate administration time—5 to 10 minutes

Scales/Scores—5

- Overall relationship satisfaction (32 items)
- Dyadic satisfaction (10 items)
- Dyadic cohesion (5 items)
- Dyadic consensus (13 items)
- Affectional expression (4 items)

Availability—The DAS is available through MHS at 908 Niagara Falls Blvd., North Tonawanda, NY 14120-2060 or through the Internet at http://www.mhs.com. The DAS is also published in Fischer and Corcoran (1994).

Cost—The paper-and-pencil DAS can be purchased for approximately $2 per couple (one form for each person), whereas computerized scoring and interpretation are available for a per-report fee.

Computer scoring—A computer scoring program can be purchased from MHS at a per-use fee (see aforementioned address). The program can be used for direct client administration or for therapist entry of the paper-and-pencil data.

Internal consistency is strong for both the total score (alpha coefficient of .96) and the subscales (range from .73 or affectional expression to .94 for dyadic satisfaction). High concurrent validity of the DAS has been found by comparing the scale to the Locke-Wallace Marital Adjustment Test. These correlations were .86 for married people and .88 for divorced people. Construct validity can be considered high as the scale reliably discriminates between divorced and married individuals (Fischer & Corcoran, 1994).

Information regarding a large number of specific instruments are available in other sources (e.g., Fischer & Corcoran, 1994; Maruish, 1999; Ogles, Lambert, & Masters, 1996; Sederer & Dickey, 1996). Many of these instruments may be useful for clinicians engaged in more narrow practices who wish to examine the effectiveness of their services for particular groups. Other types of measures are also described (e.g., therapist-rated instruments). The instruments presented here are included because they meet certain predetermined characteristics: use in therapy outcome studies, evidence of sound psychometrics, practicality, and availability of comparative data. At the same time, other promising instruments may also be useful as one begins to gather data in practice.

Of course using specific measures also presents some disadvantages. With a global measure every client entering the door can be given the measure immediately—even before visiting with a clinician. If using several specific measures, however, the clinician must meet with the person first to determine which measure should be used to assess outcome. The delay in outcome assessment that may result from first having to diagnose the client's problem may reduce the amount of therapy-related change that can be measured. Following the initial decision, the clinician must also remember which measure to administer during and after treatment to track progress. When support staff are involved in the administration of the outcome instruments, tracking which client gets which instrument could be a cumbersome task. For the global measure, no memory is required. Every client takes the same measure at every predetermined interval. In addition, using different measures requires having several scoring routines, interpretation routines, normative samples, and so on. Finally, when different measures are used, it is impossible to aggregate scores for all clients together. All reports will include different sections, a section for each group of clients completing the same measure.

In short, using multiple specific measures multiplies the data collection, interpretation, and reporting effort. This magnitude of effort is necessary and appropriate in a program of research. In most clinical settings, however, the practical hassles of using multiple specific measures outweigh the benefits of having measures that fit slightly better with the clients' problems and treatment. As a result, we recommend that clinicians use a global measure that works with the majority of clients coming into an agency or practice. A clear exception to this rule of thumb applies to the clinician who limits his or her services to a certain population. For example, a clinician who does exclusive work with individuals who have eating disorders (e.g., part-time on an inpatient unit and part-time follow-up on an outpatient basis) could use a measure or measures specific to eating disorders provided that they are sensitive to the effects of treatment. In this case, the specific instrument could be used without the hassles that go along with multiple measures in a general outpatient setting. That is, the measure(s) specific to eating disorders could be used with every client the clinician sees, and the outcome assessment protocol with a specific measure will have all the practical benefits that go along with using the global measures.

If using multiple specific measures helps to make the assessment of outcome more relevant to the individual client, the use of completely unique (i.e., individualized) outcome measures would be the ultimate in relevance.

Individualized Assessment of Outcome

A third potential content area that might be considered is the idiographic or individualized approach to assessment. In this approach, the content of the measure is unique for every client. Rather than selecting a standard global content for every client or several primary or specific content categories for the agency, the clinician tailors the outcome for every client. This approach has much appeal because it is easily integrated with treatment planning. In addition, although clearly the major complaint of a person may be summed up as anxiety, for example, this same client could have serious interpersonal problems, somatic concerns, evidence of depression, financial difficulties, marital problems, problems at work, substance abuse, and so on. These problems are often a central focus of treatment and may not be represented within global or specific-content outcome measures.

For example, Williams (1985) noted substantial variance in the kinds of situations that provoke panic across clients with Agoraphobia, including numerous phobias that appear often as simple phobias (e.g., fear of flying, heights). The typical client with Agoraphobia will usually be severely limited in some situations, moderately limited in others, and not at all restricted in other situations. In fact, the most frequent panic-provoking situation (driving on a freeway) does not cause fear for nearly 30% of individuals with Agoraphobia. Indeed Williams (1985) suggests that "[t]he configuration of fears in agoraphobics is so highly idiosyncratic that it is substantially true that no two agoraphobics have exactly the same pattern of phobias, and that two people with virtually no overlapping areas of phobia disability can both be called agoraphobic" (p. 112). As a result, the assessment of outcome using a standardized measure may overlook some important targets of treatment. It is conceivable that the client may change substantially in a given content area and the outcome measure would *not* be sensitive to that area and reflect minimal change. For this reason, some argue that individualized assessment is a preferable approach to outcome measurement. In keeping with this view, three methods of identifying individualized outcomes are presented here (target complaints, goal attainment scaling, and behavioral targets).

Target Complaints

The use of target complaints as criteria of improvement was first discussed by Battle et al. (1966). Their research suggested that target complaints were sensitive to the changes that resulted from psychotherapy and made sense to clinicians as a means to measure change. The Target Complaints method was later included in the proposed National Institute of Mental Health (NIMH) Core Battery (Waskow & Parloff, 1975). An example form is presented in Table 2.3. The measure can be used by the client, by the therapist,

Table 2.3   Example Target Complaints Rating Form

Name _____   Date _____

Therapist _____

Target Complaint #1 _____

_____

_____

_____

Severity |_____|_____|_____|_____|__

       Absent   Trivial   Mild   Moderate   Severe

Target Complaint #2 _____

_____

_____

_____

Severity |_____|_____|_____|_____|__

       Absent   Trivial   Mild   Moderate   Severe

Target Complaint #3 _____

_____

_____

_____

Severity |_____|_____|_____|_____|__

       Absent   Trivial   Mild   Moderate   Severe

or collaboratively. In each case, the individual (or therapist and client) determines the primary targets of treatment, then rates the level of severity using the simple scale (see Table 2.3).

The three target symptoms can be quite varied. They may pertain to one central problem (frequent crying, thoughts of self-harm, social isolation) or might seem to be unrelated (binge eating, social anxiety, poor work attendance). The object is to tailor the targets of treatment based on the client's presentation. Thus, neither the problems nor changes that might occur would seem irrelevant to the therapy. In fact, the therapists may state the goals of treatment in their own language and in terms of their theoretical orientation.

The clinician makes a rating after a thorough discussion of the selected target complaints. Each subsequent rating should be made without reference to initial ratings. The outcome score is the simple difference between severity ratings at intake and later ratings. These simple procedures allow the Target Complaints method to be easily applied across a broad range of clients and therapists. For clinicians who wish to use individualized approaches to outcome assessment, it may be ideal for application in a general clinical practice.

Goal Attainment Scaling

Goal attainment scaling (GAS; Kiresuk, Smith, & Cardillo, 1994; Kiresuk & Sherman, 1968) requires that a number of mental health goals be set up prior to treatment. The goals are typically agreed upon collaboratively by the client and clinician. For each goal specified, a scale with a graded series of likely outcomes, ranging from least to most favorable, is identified. These goals are formulated and specified with sufficient precision so that an independent observer could decide whether the goals were met at any given point during treatment. The procedure also allows for transformation of goal attainment into a standard score.

The procedure for evaluating goal attainment consists of six steps:

1. Goals are identified with the client.
2. Each goal is weighted according to priority.
3. A range of possible outcomes by the end of treatment is specified.
4. Current or initial level is rated.
5. Goal attainment is rated by the therapist at the end of treatment.
6. Goal attainment is evaluated either through inspection or statistical analysis. Standardized scores can be used or a weighted percentage improvement score can be calculated.

Goal attainment scaling is very flexible and can be used along with other standardized scales. In using this method for the treatment of depression, for example, one goal could be related to increased socialization. A second goal could pertain to reduction of depressive symptoms as measured by a scale such as the Beck-Depression Inventory. Further, work performance or attendance could be assessed in some form. The particular scales and behaviors examined could be varied from client to client and may include other specific definitions of improvement.

Both goal attainment and target complaints suffer from several difficulties (e.g., Mintz & Kiesler, 1982; Calsyn & Davidson, 1978).

1. Goals or complaints are judged on a relative rather than an absolute basis.
2. The goals or targets are often highly correlated, raising the issue of the need for more than one goal.
3. Goals that are too easy or difficult may prevent accurate measurement of change.
4. The attainment of goals depends in part on the therapist—progress may reflect better therapy, more modest goals, healthier clients, and so on.
5. These measures do not properly balance individualized goals with standard criteria of adjustment or progress.

Behavioral Targets

Behavior therapists and applied behavior analysts have a long tradition of identifying and monitoring target behaviors during treatment. The assessment of outcome in this instance "involves direct, quantitative measures of specific . . . behaviors, taken immediately when the behavior occurs." (p. 1; Hawkins et al., 1999). The complete details of behavior therapy (including the selection of target behaviors, intervention with the target behaviors, and the monitoring of individual change through measurement of the target behaviors) are much too lengthy to incorporate in this book, especially when the focus is on the use of standardized measures. Hawkins and colleagues (1999) produced an excellent primer on outcome assessment using the behavioral approach for clinicians involved with services for children and their families. Interested readers can seek this source and other sources if they wish to engage in a more individualized, behavioral approach to treatment and outcome assessment. Nonetheless, it is important to note that a sophisticated and elaborate body of research and clinical literature exists to guide the behavior therapist in selecting and monitoring target behaviors during treatment. The use of these methods of assessment may be equally useful for justifying treatment and gathering data for the assessment of treatment progress. At the same time, the more standardized approach to outcome assessment offers several advantages:

- The ability to compare the current client's progress with a database of progress of other similar clients
- Greater flexibility when aggregating data for the comparison of therapists, programs, or clients
- The ability to communicate with other professionals regarding the client in a standardized way (either through clinical or research-based communications)

Although we emphasize standardized assessment throughout this book, we recognize the potential benefits of individualized assessment. Indeed, we present some potential methods of incorporating a form of individualized assessment within the administration of standardized instruments. In addition, it is relatively easy to add the use of individualized assessment into an outcome system that is based on a standardized measure. For example, a therapist could administer a standardized symptom measure (such as the Brief Symptom Inventory) at each session to track a client's progress. In addition, the client and therapist could mutually agree upon two or three target problems or goals that are rated each session (e.g., target complaints, goal attainment scaling). Furthermore, the behavior therapist could track and monitor treatment specific targets for change while also administering a global measure of treatment benefit. Thus, both standardized and individualized outcome assessment can be used in tandem. Nevertheless, when resources and time are limited, our preference is to choose the standardized assessment; many of the examples presented later in the book will better illustrate this position. Rapid References 2.14 and 2.15 present some advantages and disadvantages of individualized and standardized outcome assessment.

≡*Rapid Reference 2.14*

Pros and Cons of Individualized Outcome Measurement

Pros

- Goals and targets of treatment are unique and relevant.
- The process of therapist and client selecting targets or outcomes can be therapeutic in and of itself.
- The process is easily integrated into routine treatment planning.
- Measurement can be very brief (i.e., identifying three target complaints).

Cons

- Data cannot be easily aggregated.
- It is difficult to compare the client's change with any normative or comparison group.
- It is difficult to make set decision-making protocols regarding deterioration or improvement.

≡*Rapid Reference 2.15*

Pros and Cons of Standardized Outcome Measurement

Pros

- Set protocols can be developed for administration, scoring, interpretation, and aggregation of data.
- Normative or comparison data can aid decision making.
- One instrument can be used for all clients.

Cons

- Content of items may miss unique aspects of the client's presentation.
- Length of the instrument when used repeatedly may be aversive (especially if some items are not relevant to the client).
- Forms cannot be tailored to the individual client.

SATISFACTION SURVEYS

Because the assessment of satisfaction is an important issue in many agencies, it is important to briefly address this unique content area. Many agencies are interested in gathering data regarding consumer satisfaction. As it is, satisfaction surveys may be the most practical form of "outcome" assessment. The advantages of collecting outcome data in this limited way are numerous. First, data are only collected following treatment—one time per consumer. Second, the data require relatively little time and expense to gather; satisfaction surveys can be mailed to the clients following treatment with relatively little effort. Third, the satisfaction surveys can include client retrospective ratings of improvement or benefit from treatment. Fourth, satisfaction data are generally quite favorable. The typical survey finds that 80% or more of those who respond to the survey are quite satisfied, and very few report strong dissatisfaction with treatment. Finally, many funders of services are genuinely interested in the satisfaction content area. As a result, satisfaction continues to be a prime content area for outcome assessment.

The *Consumer Reports* study is a classic example of this type of outcome assessment. This survey was conducted by the popular magazine *Consumer Reports* (*Consumer Reports,* 1995 November). The magazine staff aided by a consultant (Seligman, 1995) supplemented their annual survey with questions regarding psychotherapy and drugs. The questionnaire was given to approximately 180,000 readers, of whom 22,000 responded to the entire questionnaire and 7,000 answered the mental health questions. More than half (4,100) of the respondents to the mental health questions reported receiving assistance from some combination of mental health professionals, family doctors, or support groups, and 2,900 received services from a mental health professional. Several findings were reported (Seligman, 1995):

- Participants in mental health treatment reported benefiting from treatment.
- Longer duration of therapy was reported to be more beneficial than shorter duration of therapy.
- There were no differences between psychotherapy alone or psychotherapy plus medication.

- Psychologists, psychiatrists, and social workers performed equally well, and all of them performed better than marriage counselors.
- Family doctors performed as well as mental health professionals in the short term, but performed worse in the long term.
- People attending Alcoholics Anonymous reported the highest rates of improvement.
- Clients who carefully selected therapists and actively participated in therapy did better in treatment.
- No specific modality of therapy was more effective than any other mode of treatment.
- Clients whose therapy was limited in some manner by their insurance (e.g., choice of therapist or duration of therapy) reported less improvement.

A detailed look at the methodology and criticisms of the Consumer Reports study need not occupy these pages, but the main point is that a satisfaction survey conducted in this fashion may provide similar and sufficient information for some organizations or clinicians.

It should be noted that this type of survey has several disadvantages as well. Posttreatment satisfaction surveys have notoriously low return rates. In fact, it is not unusual to have response rates as low as 5 to 10 percent. As a result, the survey data can hardly be thought of as representative of all clients served. To get around this problem, some agencies administer satisfaction surveys to all clients receiving services for a certain time period (in a given week, for example). This data collection strategy results in a higher return rate, but it also mixes clients who have been receiving services for an extended period with those who are coming in for the first visit. In addition, the participants may still be an inadequate representation of the clients served. Posttreatment satisfaction surveys also provide little in the way of objective data regarding pretreatment to posttreatment change because they rely exclusively on the client's retrospective view of change. Gregersen et al. (2001) suggests that retrospective measures of change tend to overstate improvement and may double the effect size reported in studies that employ the usual pre-post self-report measures. In addition, posttreatment surveys with satisfaction as the primary content provide little information regarding symptomatic change. Clearly, satisfaction is poorly related to symptomatic improvement (Lunnen & Ogles, 1998). Finally, no data are available for ensuring quality or making treatment decisions during treatment when using posttreatment surveys. Failed cases discovered in a posttreatment satisfaction survey are discovered too late. Perhaps for this reason alone, we do not recommend using the satisfaction survey as the *primary* data collection strategy for clinical practice. As a *secondary* source of information regarding consumer satisfaction that supplements an ongoing clinical outcome strategy, we see no harm in gathering this type of data. Indeed, the inclusion of satisfaction data in addition to clinical outcomes adds a different and useful content area for assessment. If one must choose between the routine gathering of clinical data regarding client improvement versus satisfaction with services, however, one must choose to examine the clinical outcomes. As a result of this bias, clinical measures that give an index of the client's symptoms or functioning are highlighted throughout the book.

WHO PROVIDES THE OUTCOME INFORMATION?

Although a variety of individuals have a vested interest in the outcome of treatment, not every one can be asked to provide data regarding the outcome of service. As a result, the clinician must choose who to ask to provide information regarding treatment benefits. Strupp and Hadley (1977) presented a tripartite model of mental health outcomes. Among other things, they suggest that whether an intervention is effective depends in part upon one's perspective. They go on to suggest three primary perspectives: the client, the profession, and society. The natural tensions that exist among these perspectives influence decisions about who should report on the outcome of service.

Consumer Versus Professional

The original intervention studies relied on the therapist as the primary judge of successful treatment (Lambert, Masters, & Ogles, 1991). Later studies began to include the client as an important source of information regarding outcome. Today many research studies include multiple sources of outcome data to provide multiple perspectives. In agencies, however, the use of multiple sources may be time consuming and expensive. As a result, the delicate decision regarding the most important source is often debated. Both clients and therapists already have many demands on their time during the administration of behavioral health services. The numerous forms related to consent, billing, and treatment require substantial time and effort. When the client or therapist is asked to use even a few minutes to complete outcome data, careful thought should be given to the potential reactions to this additional paperwork.

Biased Versus Unbiased

Some have argued that the individuals involved in the intervention are biased and therefore potentially inaccurate reporters of outcome (Smith, Glass, & Miller, 1980). As a result, individuals outside of the intervention have been suggested as more objective raters of outcome. This is especially true in research regarding the efficacy of therapy. Trained observers or other raters outside the therapeutic process can be used to assess pre- and postintervention attributes in order to determine the outcome. However, the use of trained judges, significant others, teachers, and so on requires extra time, resources, and energy. In addition, these individuals have their own agendas that influence the ratings. Nevertheless, deciding whether to use participants in the intervention as the primary source of outcome assessment remains a relevant issue.

For most agencies or clinicians involved in the delivery of outpatient therapy, the frequent use of measures rated by someone other than the client or therapist is unlikely because the use of trained raters is not practical. The one exception to this rule is the use of parent-rated data for some children who are receiving individual treatment. Children's outcome assessment requires data from multiple sources (e.g., parents, youth, agency worker, and teacher; Cross et al., 1997). Especially when examining the effectiveness of services for youths with serious emotional disturbances, the involvement of multiple child-serving systems can complicate the assessment of outcome (Burchard & Shaefer, 1992). As a result, at a minimum parent ratings are almost always essential when assessing outcome of services for children. In many instances, the parent is involved in family treatment and may be considered an insider, so to speak, to the intervention anyway. Thus, obtaining parent ratings not only provides valuable information about the child, but also helps to reinforce the notion that parents are important members of the treatment team.

Institutional, Observational, or Other Nonreactive Measures of Outcome

In addition to therapist, client, and trained observer ratings of outcome, a variety of other potential sources of outcome are often collected in scientific studies. For example, heart rate data of the client when exposed to phobic stimuli, recidivism for youthful offenders, or divorce rates in marital therapy are all potential indicators of successful treatment. Some of these measures of outcome may be collected at agencies that have dedicated personnel involved in the evaluation of service effectiveness. For example, a drug and alcohol agency may examine public court records in a county of service to examine the degree to which previous clients are prosecuted at a later date. For typical outpatient providers of mental health services, however, this level of data collection may be beyond their means. In addition, this type of data rarely comes in quickly enough to inform the current ongoing treatment. Although it provides evidence of service effectiveness, it rarely changes or corrects ongoing treatment. As a result, further examination of this type of outcome evaluation is not considered. Essential outcome assessment for the outpatient provider requires input from the client.

Recommendations Regarding Who Should Assess Outcome

As is clearly evident in the selection of instruments presented earlier in this chapter, we present almost exclusively instruments for adults that are self-report. For children, we rely heavily on self- and parent-report instruments. Although numerous therapist- or judge-rated instruments are available, these instruments have several problems that limit their utility:

- Most payors want to know whether their customers are satisfied and benefit from treatment. The payors are not impressed when the therapist indicates the client has changed if the client does not see the same improvement or is dissatisfied with treatment. For example, if an employee of XYZ company seeks treatment through the company's contractual Employee Assistance Program, the XYZ executive who oversees the contract will be more interested in data driven by the employee's ratings of change or satisfaction than in the therapist's ratings of change. Payors view the contractual agency therapist ratings of improvement as potentially motivated by financial incentives and by the desire to renew the contract.
- Therapist-rated outcome measures require more paperwork from the clinician. With the exceptional paperwork requirements already in existence, adding more work for the clinician seems impractical, especially given our first point.
- Judge-rated outcome measures cannot be implemented practically in clinical settings. In a research protocol, the client may participate in an independent interview with a trained clinician who rates the level of functioning or symptoms of the client prior to and following treatment. In most clinical settings, however, it is not practical to use client time or another clinician's time in this way.
- Self-report measures are of-

> **DON'T FORGET**
>
> The consumer's perspective of his or her benefit from treatment is likely to be the most helpful for tracking change and creating reports to be viewed by external sources. The therapist perspective is sometimes viewed with skepticism because of the potential for bias. Other sources of outcome data (e.g., recidivism rates, teacher ratings) may be difficult to collect.

ten inexpensive, easy to administer, and versatile. Similarly, they can be readily applied in a variety of mental health settings, such as outpatient clinics, schools, and physicians' offices.

- Self-report measures give the consumer's view of the presenting problems and progress in treatment. This issue is particularly important given the current consumer empowerment movement.
- The therapeutic alliance may be enhanced by allowing clients an opportunity to share their voices through self-report measures (Eisen, Leff, & Schaefer, 1999).
- For assuring quality and providing feedback to therapists regarding client improvement, it is absolutely necessary to provide them with information to which they do not already have access—that is, the client's perspective of improvement.

SUMMARY

When selecting instruments for the assessment of clinical outcomes in outpatient behavioral health services, the typical clinician wants information to inform the current treatment, aggregate for internal reporting, and summarize for external reporting (e.g., marketing). Although a variety of outcome measurement methods and instruments have been used in research, the presentation of primarily global, client-rated measures is central to this chapter in order to meet the outpatient clinician's needs in a practical way. In addition to presenting a categorical and conceptual scheme for categorizing outcome measures, outcome measures that are ready for applied use have been selected and described in order to facilitate the selection of appropriate instruments.

The consideration of the pros and cons of other options is presented in the event that some clinicians prefer the alternatives (e.g., individualized outcome assessment approaches). The remaining chapters illustrate the methods for using global, client-rated instruments in practice. Remaining issues include how and when to administer the instruments (i.e., setting up the data collection routine), how to use the data after they are gathered, and examples of the procedures that are described.

1. **Which of the following should one bear in mind when selecting an out-come measure?**

   (a) The audience

   (b) The trade-offs of assessing various content areas

   (c) Resource limitations

   (d) All of the above

   (e) None of the above

2. **What is the biggest practical advantage of global measures of outcome as-sessment?**

   (a) They can be administered to every client.

   (b) They are clinically sound instruments.

   (c) They lend themselves well to aggregation.

   (d) They can be shaped to fit the needs of individual clients.

   (e) Norm groups can be compared to individual clients.

3. **Which of the following is a global measure of outcome assessment?**

   (a) Beck Depression Inventory

   (b) State-Trait Anxiety Inventory

   (c) Dyadic Adjustment Questionnaire

   (d) All of the above

   (e) None of the above

4. **Which of the following is a specific measure of outcome assessment?**

   (a) Outcome Questionnaire—45

   (b) Fear Questionnaire

   (c) Child Behavior Checklist

   (d) Symptom Checklist 90—Revised

   (e) All of the above

5. **In which of the following settings would a clinician be most justified in using a specific measure of outcome assessment?**

   (a) Eating disorders clinic

   (b) Outpatient mental health clinic

   (c) Community counseling center

   (d) Inpatient unit

   (e) Day treatment program

(continued)

6. Outcome assessment for youth poses unique problems for researchers and clinicians because unlike adult measures,

(a) youth measures are not normed.

(b) youth measures are not informative.

(c) there is a scarcity of youth measures.

(d) there is an abundance of youth measures.

(e) youth measures cannot be completed by the client.

7. Which of the following is a drawback of the individualized approach to assessment?

(a) The process of selecting outcomes and targets is too cumbersome.

(b) The manner of assessment is too brief and thus not useful.

(c) Statistical procedures involved with this method are too lengthy.

(d) It is difficult to aggregate data generated from this method.

(e) It is difficult to integrate into routine treatment planning.

8. Client satisfaction surveys tend to be favorable for mental health treatment, and it is not unusual for response rates to be

(a) 50%.

(b) 80%.

(c) 25%.

(d) 90% or more.

(e) 10% or less.

9. If only one perspective on adult client outcome can be gathered, which is the most important?

(a) Clinician

(b) Client

(c) Family member

(d) Trained observer

(e) Employer

Answers: 1. d; 2. a; 3. e; 4. b; 5. a; 6. c; 7. d; 8. e; 9. b

Three

SETTING UP DATA COLLECTION PROCEDURES

As highlighted in Chapter 2, clinicians can choose from a vast array of instruments to evaluate treatment outcome for mental health clients. The advantages and disadvantages of various test instruments continue to be argued in both the treatment of adults and of children, but the fact remains that numerous practical scales with excellent psychometric properties and normative data are available. Regardless of which outcome instrument is best suited for a given mental health setting, the procedure utilized to gather the outcome data is paramount in determining the success of outcome assessment. To reinforce an old cliché, in the world of outcome assessment, the devil is truly in the details.

After the outcome measure or battery of instruments is selected, the task for practitioners shifts toward establishing a procedure or routine for the collection of outcome data. Those who oversee outcome assessment in real-world clinic settings have the arduous task of developing and maintaining a routine set of procedures for gathering the outcome data. The procedures need to be clear and consistent, but it is also true that some clients may have special needs (e.g., illiteracy) that make it impossible to follow the standard procedure devised for a clinic site. In these situations, modifications may need to be made from the typical procedure so that data can still be obtained and useful information about the individual can be gleaned from the assessment.

Even when the decision is made to collect a specific type of outcome assessment data, numerous questions about the testing procedure can still arise. The answers to these questions can vary widely depending on the type of service delivered, the clientele, and other situational circumstances (Mordock, 2000). Thus, different circumstances call for varied procedures. This chapter provides some answers to questions regarding when and how to collect the outcome assessment data. In keeping with our running theme, the advantages and disadvantages of various approaches are explored and recommendations evolving from the presumed world of the typical outpatient service provider are offered. As a result, rather than presenting an elaborate model of data collection that is based on a battery of instruments specific to various client groups, we focus on the procedures that may be most useful for gathering data using a single, client-rated, global measure of outcome.

WHEN TO GATHER INTAKE DATA?

Once the measure is selected, the first procedural question is when the client will complete the instrument. Two related questions are central. First, at what point during the initial and subsequent visits does the client complete the scale (before, during, or after the visit)? Second, how often does the client complete the scale (end of treatment only, pre- and post-treatment, at regular intervals)?

At What Point During the Visit?

When a new client makes a phone call to set up an appointment or walks into a clinic, at what point should he or she be introduced to the outcome assessment instrument and asked to complete it? If a global measure is used that can be completed by every client, the outcome instrument can be easily included with other initial paperwork such as billing and contact information. If more than one measure is used, then some contact with an intake worker or other decision-maker must occur in order to determine which measure is most appropriate for the client. Our recommendation is to give the client the measure as soon as possible in the first appointment or prior to the appointment. At the first appointment, the gathering of basic clinical information in an intake interview may not seem especially therapeutic, but clients often experience some relief as a result of meeting with a clinician, sharing the reason for coming in, and setting up regular appointments to begin dealing with the issues. Indeed, the hope that is gained from these initial meetings may be the most central ingredient to client change (Howard et al., 1996). In addition, it would not be unusual for the clinician to begin treatment during the intake interview. Finally, it is well known that client change occurs more rapidly during early sessions than in later sessions (Anderson & Lambert, 2001; Barkham et al., 1996; Howard, Kopta, Krause, & Orlinsky, 1986; Kadera, Lambert, & Andrews, 1996). As a result, an outcome measure that is administered after the intake session may miss significant change that occurs as a result of the initial appointment. In short, the sooner the client can complete the outcome instrument, the more likely you are to capture all change that occurs during his or her participation in services. As a result, we recommend administering the instrument as soon as it is practical within the normal paperwork processes. (Incidentally, the benefits of administering the instrument earlier are also a reason for choosing a global measure that can be given to every client. With a single measure, the client could be asked to complete the measure immediately upon arriving at the office.) More is discussed later in this chapter regarding how to administer the measure when the client arrives.

Similarly, we recommend that when the outcome measure is administered at subsequent visits, it should be administered prior to the session. In this way, the client can rate his or her current level of symptoms or functioning while considering the week since the most recent appointment and prior to participating in the therapeutic process. This also avoids the possibility of biased or reactive outcome ratings— ratings that are influenced by reviewing problematic experiences

CAUTION

....

Although we recommend administering the instrument early in the intake process in order to capture all of the change that occurs during treatment, the lack of proper controls prevents the attribution of change to treatment. The changes that occur early in treatment may or may not be related to our theories of the hope that is engendered by the process of the intake. Appropriate, randomly controlled studies would be needed to test the degree to which the intake itself causes the change that occurs from the time before the appointment to the time after the appointment.

during the session and arousing or diminishing distressing emotions or thoughts. Finally, client ratings prior to the session raise the possibility of providing the therapist with feedback regarding client progress in the opening moments of the session. This feedback may serve as a stimulus for therapeutic work or guidance regarding potential topics for treatment.

At What Interval?

A more difficult practical issue involves the decisions regarding how often to administer the instrument(s). Every administration requires an assigned person who must (a) remember to gather the data, (b) collect the data, (c) score or enter the data for scoring, and so forth. In addition, for many instruments, each administration comes with some expense. As a result, many practical issues press for fewer administrations. At the same time, the more frequent the data are collected, the more information the clinician has regarding client progress. Similarly, a few practical reasons support more frequent data gathering. For the typical outpatient therapist or agency, the primary options include (a) gathering data one time retrospectively following treatment, (b) gathering data at the beginning and end of treatment, or (c) gathering data at some predetermined interval (e.g., every session, every third session, etc.) from the beginning to the end of treatment.

Prospective Versus Retrospective

One important dichotomy that exists is whether data should be gathered prospectively or retrospectively. As illustrated earlier using the *Consumer Reports* survey, some agencies send out posttreatment satisfaction surveys to clients. This retrospective data gathering can include client ratings of satisfaction with services, current level of distress, and ratings of perceived improvement. A clear advantage to this type of data collection is that it need only be collected once, at some predetermined point at the end of treatment or soon after services end. As a result, the cost and time needed to gather one set of data from each client may be quite reasonable. Unfortunately, there are many disadvantages to retrospective data collection. Attrition rates in treatment are quite high. The modal number of sessions attended is one, and typically 50% of clients have departed from services by the fifth session (Garfield, 1994). As a result many clients may not attend a final session in which they can make retrospective ratings. In this case, retrospective data may only be representative of clients who continue in therapy for extended periods of time or who are more faithful in attendance. It seems unlikely that the clinician would not want to hear from those clients who complete therapy sooner or neglect to attend some sessions, especially because a large number of clients gained substantive relief that is maintained (Haas, Hill, Lambert, & Morrell, in press). If retrospective data are collected via a posttreatment mailed survey, return rates are notoriously low. As a result, retrospective ratings rarely provide an accurate picture of the entire body of clients served. Rather, the most unhappy, disgruntled clients and the most pleased and satisfied clients are also the ones most likely to respond to retrospective surveys, making the survey less useful for agencies. The pros and cons of retrospective data collection are summarized in Rapid Reference 3.1.

In contrast to the proponents of retrospective data, some prefer to gather information at the time of intake so that they can compare the as-

≡*Rapid Reference 3.1*

Pros and Cons of Retrospective Data Collection

Pros
- Requires only one data collection point from each client
- Less expensive
- Less time consuming

Cons
- High attrition rates in treatment or poor survey response rates reduce the number of clients who participate
- No objective data regarding pre- and posttreatment change
- No comparison against a standard of health or clinical status
- No timely information during treatment to provide feedback or to influence the course of treatment

sessment at that time to functioning at other points during treatment. This prospective data can portray actual changes in symptom severity occurring over time rather than relying on the client's memory of pretreatment functioning. The measures used in this type of outcome assessment are generally standardized so that meaningful comparisons can be made from one point in time to another and with other comparison samples. Of course, prospective data must be obtained at multiple times during treatment and therefore greater energy, effort, and cost are needed to keep track of data points throughout the duration of treatment. Practically, it may be easier for agencies to gather data retrospectively after treatment has been provided. On the other hand, prospective data can provide the clinician with in-the-moment information regarding client progress from intake to the current session. This information arrives in time to modify treatment and thus can be helpful for both the therapist and the client. Similarly, prospective data gives more objective evidence of client improvement (or deterioration) because the scores from before treatment and later in treatment can be compared to one another and to those of a norm group. Finally, prospective data collection may eliminate some of the problems with poor survey response rates or attrition. As a result of these distinct advantages, prospective data collection is preferable.

Pre-Post or Multiple Time Points?

If the decision is made to collect data at more than one time during the treatment of a client, then a separate issue surfaces regarding how often data should be collected. There are various opinions about how often an instrument should be used to assess outcome in mental health treatment. For example, the Ohio Department of Mental Health currently requires periodic outcome assessment for individuals receiving state-funded mental health services. The mandated outcome assessment includes the completion of measures at intake, six months after intake, and then every year thereafter or upon completion of service, whichever comes first (Ohio Department of Mental Health, 2000). This type of assessment is clearly geared toward individuals who are likely to participate in services over a long period of time. For those receiving outpatient services for acute mental health issues, the typical administration points would be at intake and at the end of treatment. In fact, because of the costs associated with more frequent assessment, some clinicians prefer preintervention and postintervention assessments only.

The advantages to pre-post assessment are the limited amount of data collection (two time points), sufficient data are gathered to gauge the degree to which the client benefited from treatment, and data can be easily aggregated for pre-to-post estimates of change. One of the hassles of pre-post data collection is the problem of determining when the end of treatment will occur so that the instrument can be administered. Because the therapist is the most likely to know when the client will finish treatment, the job of administering the posttreatment measure typically falls in the hands of the therapist and may not be easily delegated to office staff. Thus, more responsibility falls into the hands of the therapist with this method of assessment.

Prospective data gathering, although it has the advantage of being able to demonstrate change in treatment, is often stymied by the large number of people who drop out before a second outcome assessment. Obviously, pre-post data collection would include only those clients who completed treatment or have willingly decided to drop out (e.g., the therapist knows they are not coming back and therefore administers the instrument at that point in time). For those who drop out before an agreed-upon end to treatment, posttreatment data may be difficult to gather and may also introduce a burden to the therapist. Thus, if a client is being assessed every sixth session, then the chances of a dropout's interfering with a second data point in treatment are larger than they would be if that client were assessed every session. Client dropout becomes a much greater obstacle when periodic assessments are given. Dropout from treatment is a plague for psychotherapy researchers, who routinely deal with the problems of analyzing data in which many participants did not complete the treatment or the data collection. Dropout is also a frequent problem in outpatient settings (Wierzbicki & Pekarik, 1993). As a result, prepost assessment will of necessity be limited to approximately 50 to 75% of clients who are receiving services, with many of those who are excluded showing the greatest gains

(Haas et al., in press). Attempts to remedy this problem through mail or telephone contact may increase the rate of participation, but increase the costs associated with gathering the data and will not entirely resolve the attrition and response rate problems.

In addition, the end point, or postintervention assessment, will certainly be different from client to client. Thus, outcomes may be compared among people who have only been in treatment for a few sessions versus people who have been in treatment for several years. Clinicians must be careful not to compare the therapy equivalent of apples and oranges, or individuals who have been in treatment a long time versus individuals who have only received brief, acute treatment. At the same time, some statistical methods of examining this data are available.

It will also be important to determine when posttreatment actually begins. Is it immediately following the last session? Should it be when one type of service is discontinued or when all services are stopped? These are important questions to consider. In general, posttreatment can refer to the end of a specific type of treatment. For example, if a client is released from therapy and continues to see the psychiatrist for medication monitoring, it would be appropriate for the therapist to administer an outcome assessment instrument because the treatment that he or she provided is no longer being administered.

But the most important criticism of the pre-post method of examining treatment is that the data are not available to modify treatment! As we highlight in the chapters to come, outcome data can be of great benefit to therapists so that they can plan current treatment and make modifications to existing treatment on a patient-by-patient basis. The pre-post method simply verifies or documents the degree to which clients benefited from treatment as they are walking out the door. If they are worse, the data arrive far too late to intervene effectively. As a result, we recommend that the data be gathered at more frequent intervals. In fact, our preferred method of gathering outcome data is to ask the client to complete the instrument just prior to every session (Lambert, Hansen, & Finch, 2001; Lambert, Okiishi, Finch, & Johnson, 1998). Let us explain why.

Although data to inform treatment may be gathered at intervals less frequent than every session, several practical problems can be solved by every-session administration. When selecting intervals less frequent than every session (e.g., every third), someone must keep track of when to administer the instrument. For every client coming in the door, someone must decide—What session is this? And, is it the time to administer the instrument? Although these are simple questions, keeping track of this information for a large pool of clients can be exceptionally difficult and will ultimately result in missed data collection, especially when a specific measure is used by different clients. In contrast, when data are gathered at every session there are no questions to ask. A stack of measures can be placed on a desk in the lobby and all clients can be socialized to the fact that they should take the appropriate measure as soon as they arrive for every session. No one need determine who must complete the measure because all should do it. In short, the administration of the instrument to every client at every session eliminates the need to make decisions regarding when and who should complete the instrument.

In addition to this practical benefit, the every-session administration handles problems with attrition. If every client completes the measure every session, then automatically every client's data up to his or her final session (i.e., the end of treatment) will be collected. Even clients who drop out of treatment will have the most recent data for their final session. As a result, there can be a substantial increase in the number of clients who have data from the first to final session of their outpatient therapy. Indeed, one very interesting analysis might compare those clients who drop out without informing the therapist versus those who finish treatment via an agreed closure with the therapist. Because many clients participate in outpatient therapy for just a few sessions, the total number of data points per client will actually be small. Only a few (typically 10%) clients will have a long duration of treatment requiring multiple administrations of the instrument.

Repeated assessments also make it possible to compare clients who have received services in the same time frame with one another. For example, data on all individuals who have received services for six weeks can be aggregated. Thus, the problem of variable end points on the evaluation is eliminated, and clients with similar treatment profiles can be compared.

Assessing client outcome at every session has the distinct advantage of continuous feedback throughout the treatment process; benefits of this assessment method are outlined in Rapid Reference 3.2. Response to therapy could be monitored from one session to the next and charted by clinicians. Furthermore, this information could not only be used by therapists, but also by the clients so that they could note progress toward goals and work on positive behavioral change. Of course, the drawback to assessment after every session is the time, energy, and cost that would go into completing forms every session. Depending on the specific measure, a large amount of time and energy might be spent completing outcome assessment forms. Some clinicians might also be concerned about client fatigue in response to having to complete the scales before every encounter with the clinician. However, this cost in time and energy could be offset by the usage of a brief, focused outcome assessment instrument. Another drawback is that if a measure is given over and over at each session, a client might be more likely to drift into a response set, or a pattern of answering questions in a certain way time after time. Helping the client to understand the benefits of careful rating up front, and monitoring client responses, can prevent this type of response bias.

McGlynn (1996) also points out the importance of expected rate of change

≡Rapid Reference 3.2

The Benefits of Every-Session Administration

- Eliminates confusion about who should complete the measure at what specific time because all take it every time.
- Eliminates problems with attrition because every client will complete the instrument prior to the final session whether he or she drops out or ends collaboratively.
- Provides session-by-session data for continuous monitoring of treatment progress and potential quality assurance.
- Allows for frequent assessment of change, which is particularly important in the early sessions of treatment.

and outcome attributions in treatment. McGlynn writes, "In determining the optimal time frame for outcome assessments, the expected rate of change in outcomes for the intervention being evaluated and the anticipated attribution of outcomes should be considered" (1996, p. 19). As already noted, in outpatient psychotherapy, substantial data demonstrate that most of the benefits of treatment occur in the early sessions (Lambert & Ogles, in press). As a result, every session administration would be especially important early in treatment. The clinician who administers outcome instruments only after a set number of sessions (e.g., six sessions) runs the risk of overlooking substantial gains that might be made in the early treatment sessions.

Follow-Up or Not?

A final issue that may be considered when addressing when to conduct outcome assessment is the need for follow-up assessment. Whereas postintervention assessments provide valuable information about treatment efficacy, follow-up data can also provide evidence of lasting change well after therapy has ended. Follow-up data, by definition, can be gathered at any time after treatment is finished. However, it is often more useful to gather follow-up data at least a few months after treatment so that the lasting effects of treatment can be demonstrated. As with prior arguments about the appropriate time intervals, there is no agreed-upon answer regarding what an appropriate follow-up period would be.

Studies of psychotherapy efficacy would not be complete without data demonstrating that client improvement extends beyond the end of treatment. If clients continue to function well after treatment has ended, then this lends important evidence to the idea that the benefits of psychotherapy are long-standing. When evaluating treatment benefits in an outpatient setting, however, the costs associated with keeping track of clients to gather follow-up data are tremendous. Indeed, the costs associated with such a practice certainly outweigh the benefits of the data that might be gathered. The largest drawback to gathering data at these time periods is that it is often difficult to locate clients after treatment has been terminated. Clients move, telephone numbers change, and relevant contact information about clients

DON'T FORGET

For most outpatient therapy settings, the gathering of long-term follow-up data would not be practical and is considered a luxury, whereas it is essential in well-controlled research studies.

may be lost after many months. Furthermore, the response rate for follow-ups can be exceedingly low. As a result, our recommendation is that for most outpatient service delivery agencies, follow-up data are not a high priority and should not be collected. For the researcher trying to demonstrate the efficacy of a specific treatment, follow-up is a necessity. For most practitioners, however, follow-up data are a luxury that they can ill afford.

A Final Word on When to Gather Data

In making a decision about when to gather outcome assessment data, clinicians and administrators should consider the real-world limitations that face them. The practical constraints of employee time, data flow, and consumer reaction to repeated administration of the same outcome measures will be pivotal in determining which procedure to use. In summary, although the decision of how often outcome assessment should occur is open to discussion, one-time assessments are less useful clinically than are repeated measures, and every-session administration is more useful than periodic assessment. Data collected at every session can be used to track client changes, to monitor progress, and eventually to manage treatment quality. At the same time, instruments that will be administered numerous times will need to be more practical and less time consuming than instruments that will be used less frequently, such as an intake-only measure. Brief, easy-to-score measures are ideal to help clinicians monitor client treatment and potentially help them manage the care of a client.

HOW TO COLLECT OUTCOME DATA?

The specific details of test administration change based on the type of instrument or battery that is utilized. Because we emphasize global, client-report measures of change, our focus will remain on the administration procedures for such instruments. Clinicians who select other instruments, such as therapist- or rater-based instruments, will need to carefully consider additional issues. For example, in an agency that decides to collect clinician-rated outcome, the probability of clinician turnover will likely result in a situation in which one clinician rates the client at intake and another one rates the client at a later point in time. As a result, the interrater reliability of the measure must be considered. Importantly, the manual for each specific test instrument should be consulted to help guide the administration. In addition, books that combine various measures such as *The Sourcebook of Adult Assessment Strategies* (Schutte & Malouff, 1995) can be quite helpful in providing administration procedures for a number of scales. For most self-report instruments, however, simple written instructions are sufficient for the large majority of people who complete the form.

One area of importance in test administration is the examiner's familiarity with the instrument being utilized (Gregory, 1996). An examiner must have some facility with the test instruments being used and with any equipment that needs to be used during the evaluation. Many outcome measures include various technologies for gathering the data (e.g., scannable forms, internet data entry, telephone entry). As a result, clinicians need to be familiar with the methods that will be used to gather the data in their practice or agency. Errors in test administration can lead to inaccurate findings for test-takers and to poor treatment decisions by clinicians. Ultimately, these errors can be costly for clients if they do not receive the appropriate treatment because of recommendations garnered from a flawed assessment.

In contrast to other more elaborate instruments that are used for psychological assessment, outcome questionnaires tend to be easy to administer. Nonetheless, clinicians still need to be vigilant in order to minimize the likelihood of errors in administration or scoring. Using the principles suggested in Chapter 2, however, the clinician should have already selected an appropriate measure for his or her typical clientele. The remaining concern, then, is the protocol for administering the instrument. We get to this issue shortly.

DON'T FORGET

The clinician needs to be familiar with the outcome assessment instrument, the technology available for the instrument, and the appropriate conditions under which the instrument should be used or not used. Special attention should be given to situations that may require deviations from the typical administration (e.g., assistance with reading).

One often overlooked yet important area of outcome assessment is the establishment of rapport with the client being assessed (Davis, Meagher, Goncalves, Woodward, & Millon, 1999). Rapport can be defined as a comfortable, warm atmosphere established by the examiner that helps elicit cooperation and motivation from examinees. An examiner can establish rapport by generating discussion with the examinee before the assessment procedure begins. The principles associated with appropriate rapport in other psychological assessment situations (e.g., personality assessment, diagnostic assessment, or intellectual assessment) are well known. For example, Wechsler (1974) suggested that with children, an examinee might discuss a child's hobbies or interests for a few minutes before the formal assessment begins. It is also common to maintain rapport by providing occasional positive comments at certain times during the evaluation, provided it does not interfere with the standard administration procedures. For outcome assessment, rapport can also be important, especially when the clinician requests that the client complete the measure at every session. Helping the client to understand the purpose of the frequent assessment, using the data in the session (so the client understands how the data can be helpful), and occasional reminders or expressions of gratitude for the clients' willingness to complete the forms will help eliminate potential problems associated with repeated assessment.

The amount of rapport that needs to be established will likely

DON'T FORGET

Even in simple outcome assessments, the establishment of rapport, or a comfortable, warm atmosphere for the patient, is important. Establishing and maintaining rapport are especially important when administering the instruments repeatedly over time.

vary depending on the tests being administered. A simple question-naire may require only a few words of encouragement or instruction at the onset. Importantly, outcome assessment will often be adminis-tered by support staff in agencies with a reception area and recep-tionist. As a result, training sup-port staff regarding the tone and

> **DON'T FORGET**
>
> Because support staff will often ad-minister outcome questionnaires, it will be necessary to train them re-garding the importance of the as-sessment, the appropriate adminis-tration and scoring of the tests, and a positive tone about their im-portance.

type of instructions to provide the client will be especially important. A tester who does not establish rapport with a client runs the risk of induc-ing anxiety, hostility, or passive-aggression on the part of examinees (Gre-gory, 1996). These variables have the potential to affect performance or re-sponses to test items, and nonrepresentative findings could be the end result of failing to properly establish rapport. Thus, although a minimal amount of rapport needs to be established with brief questionnaires, if the atmosphere is hurried or hostile, it could affect the responses of the client.

The testing environment is another important variable that can some-times be overlooked when considering outcome administration. Because the client will typically be completing the measure prior to the session, while waiting for the appointment to begin, adequate lighting, space, privacy, and absence of distractions will help the client focus. In fact, it may be helpful to have a table available in the waiting room so that forms can be filled out comfortably. Procedures for maintaining confidentiality of the data also need to be considered, and raw data must not be kept in places where other clients could find it. In summary, an adequate testing environment is one in which the client can feel relatively comfortable and can complete the out-come measure with a minimum of visual and auditory distractions.

Receptionist or Clinician?

Another issue to consider when considering outcome procedures is decid-ing who gathers the data. Should it be the clinician or clerical staff, or should it be done via mail or telephone survey? In keeping with our every-session administration prior to the actual therapy, the most logical person to administer the instrument is a support staff member. Clients typically complete a number of forms prior to their first visit with a clinician. As a result, including the outcome measure with this packet of forms is a simple way to obtain initial data. The receptionist or staff member who assists with the packet can give a brief explanation of the need for assessment data. When the clinician meets with the client, the clinician can give a more detailed explanation including instructions regarding the need to complete the measure prior to every session. Perhaps the preferred method of handling the assessment at subsequent sessions would be to ask the receptionist to give the outcome measure to the client when he or she checks in for the appointment. When the client has completed the instrument, then the receptionist notifies the therapist that the client has arrived. Of course some individual practitioners will have an office without support staff. In this case, the clinician can give a simple explanation to the client prior to the first visit as the client completes initial forms. The clinician might also put a stack of outcome measures in the waiting room. The clinician can then instruct the client to come a few minutes prior to each session, get the form, and complete it prior to the session. The completed form can then either be given to the therapist or placed in a locked box for later scoring and perusal.

CAUTION

When the use of the outcome data extends beyond the monitoring of individual client progress (i.e., uses that are not related to a client's individual treatment), the clinician should consider adding a consent form to the intake; this consent form informs the client regarding the potential uses of the data and obtains the client's consent for participation.

Consent Form or Not?

An important issue that should not be overlooked is whether to have the client complete a research consent form related to the gathering of outcome data. When the outcome assessment data are gathered to inform treatment, the typical consent for treatment forms cover the gathering and use of any assessment data. If the clinician plans to use the data for other purposes (e.g., publication or presentation) or if the data gathered are part of a larger evaluation or research procedure, then a separate consent form that informs the client of the potential uses of the data and the evaluation procedures may be necessary.

Youth Self-Report

The administration of child self-report measures varies more than adult measures and may require some consideration of additional issues. As mentioned earlier, outcome assessment for child and adolescent services often requires the gathering of data from more than one source. Especially for adolescents, the clinician will want, at a minimum, both the child and parent perspective. Teacher report of outcome may be necessary in some circumstances. Indeed, several multisource measures of outcome are available for assessing outcome of behavioral health services for youth (e.g., CBCL, Ohio Scales; Rapid Reference 3.3 describes some features of multisource outcome assessment). At the same time, our most practical recommendation would be to use a parent-rated global outcome measure for all youth. Again, the pragmatics of having one scale available for all youth clients eliminates the practical hassles associated with matching instruments to clients.

Reading levels for children also vary significantly. As a result, the clinician needs to be aware of the child's ability to participate in the outcome data assessment without assistance. Since children and adolescents often have a more difficult time holding their attention to a task, most scales for youth should be briefer than adult scales. Similarly, they may require more hands-on assistance or encouragement during completion of the measures. Practical difficulties arise when parents are expected to

≡Rapid Reference 3.3

Multisource Outcome Assessment

Multisource outcome assessment has the advantages of offering various points of view regarding the benefits of treatment. Multiple perspectives are more necessary for services with children and youth. Nevertheless, the parent is typically the primary informant, and a reliance on parent-rated outcome may be the most practical method of assessing outcome with the child and adolescent population.

complete the measure each session, but they prefer to drop off the youth for the appointment or send the child to the session without attending themselves. As a result, gathering parent data will be more difficult and could require additional efforts (e.g., asking the child to take the measure home and bring it back the next session or completing the ratings over the phone). Prior studies have found discrepancies in how parents and children view a child's pathology (Achenbach, McConaughty, & Howell, 1987). As a result, parent and youth data may present a puzzling clinical interpretive problem.

TEST SCORING

After the client has completed the outcome measure, scoring, data entry, and use of the data are the subsequent steps. Because numerous types of tests are available, it stands to reason that many different issues could arise when the clinician is scoring tests used for outcome assessment. Tests with true-or-false formats are often the easiest to score, whereas projective measures (which are rarely used for outcome assessment) can be quite difficult to score for clinicians. One general rule in scoring tests is that the examiner be highly familiar with the scoring procedure. The amount of practice and preparation that goes into scoring outcome measures varies depending on the difficulty of the instrument being used. Some simple, brief instruments can be scored with relative ease (e.g., OQ-45), whereas others have more complicated scoring procedures (e.g., CBCL). Staying abreast of scoring procedures is important. At a bare minimum, it is necessary to read the administration manual of the outcome measure so that one can learn how to score the test properly. Familiarity with the outcome measure will help ensure that the test results obtained are indeed valid indicators of the examinee's functioning.

In this age of computers, many agencies may develop or purchase computerized scoring algorithms.

CAUTION

Clinicians have a responsibility to keep abreast of current scoring practices on various outcome assessment instruments. They should be familiar with both the instrument and the administration manual so that mistakes are minimized.

For example, some may gather data using a scannable entry form, point-of-view entry box, or telephone voice response system. These data-gathering systems allow direct entry of the data into computer databases and make possible the immediate printout of reports. The computer does the work of summing the totals and scale scores and produces printouts of profiles and comparisons with normative data. However, it is imperative that clinicians not fall into the trap of assuming that computer-generated data are automatically reliable. If examinees fail to darken in ovals sufficiently on scoring sheets, or if they make stray marks through items they did not intend to endorse, the data that result from these errors will invalidate the assessment. In order to keep such an error from occurring, Gregory (1996) recommended that someone inspect data sheets before submitting them for scoring. In particular, one should look for missing data, stray marks, or irregularities in the filling out of the measures.

Even without these sophisticated technologies, however, most of the global, self-report instruments presented in Chapter 2 could be quickly scored by an office worker or the clinician prior to the session. This makes it possible to use the data in the session so that client progress can be discussed. The agency must determine the typical routine for scoring. Whether the data are scored by the clinician or a staff worker is less important than having a set routine, accurate scoring, and a procedure for entering the data into a database for aggregate analysis and reporting. Protocol is outlined in Rapid Reference 3.4.

The issue of examiner variance, or differences in scoring among various examiners, is a key topic. If examiners do not score outcome measures in similar ways, then the results are definitely less meaningful and helpful for clinicians and clients. Anastasi (1988) wrote that "most tests provide such highly standardized procedures for administration and scoring that error variance attributable to these factors (following directions) is negligible" (p. 125). This seems especially true for measures that are scored by computer, provided the examiner inspects the profiles for stray marks and inconsistencies. Scoring errors are not as big a problem as some might think. Although some items might be scored incorrectly, most mistakes in scoring tend to balance out so that one item might be scored too high and the next too low. Clerical scoring errors, however, appear to be a more perva-

≈ *Rapid Reference 3.4*

Typical Outcome Assessment Administration Protocol

1. Client comes a few minutes early to the appointment.
2. The receptionist gives the client the instrument to complete prior to the session.
3. Once the instrument is completed, the receptionist quickly scores it (either via technology or template).
4. The clinician is notified of the client's arrival.
5. When the clinician comes to the waiting room, the clinician picks up the scored outcome measure to review (either for information or use in the session).
6. Each patient chart includes a graph for tracking scores over time. The clinician uses the outcome data to chart the next data point and examine client progress.
7. Either earlier when scored or following the session, the client outcome data are entered into a database for later aggregation of data.

sive and dangerous problem for examiners. Gregory (1987) reports on one study in which a group of advanced graduate students erred by as many as 30 IQ points when scoring a standard IQ test protocol! Clerical scoring errors were believed to be the culprit in this study, and Gregory concluded that errors of this type threaten the integrity of the measures being used to assess examinees. The only sure way to avoid these types of errors is for examiners to use caution when scoring outcome instruments and for scorers to double-check their work once they are finished. Although carefully scrutinizing one's work can be tedious, it is a far better annoyance than finding out one has erroneously scored a test and subsequently reached the wrong conclusions about a client.

SUMMARY

One certain thing about outcome assessment is that it can vary greatly from one treatment site to the next, or even from one clinician to the next. Various tensions influence the decisions regarding who the informant should be, how outcome assessment should be done, and when data should be collected. No single method of outcome is perfect, as trade-offs exist whenever a decision is made to gather data at a particular time or from a particular informant. While considering the tensions that exist when doing outcome assessment, we make the following summary recommendations.

> ## CAUTION
>
> The only sure way to avoid clerical errors is to use caution when scoring instruments and to double-check the math after the scoring is completed. The use of computerized technology will eliminate some common clerical errors, but also increases the possibility of data entry error.

1. Gather data before each and every session.
2. Consider the testing environment (e.g., lighting) and remember that good rapport will help keep the client motivated to complete the measure multiple times.
3. Develop a consistent routine for administering, scoring, using, and entering the data into a database.
4. The routines should handle the administration and scoring quickly enough to allow for the use of the data in ongoing treatment. The provision of immediate feedback and practical, understandable results for clients and family members is also important (Newman et al., 1999).
5. Routines may need to be modified for individuals with special needs (e.g., those who need assistance with reading) or certain populations (e.g., children—seeking parent reported outcome).
6. Aggregate data analysis and reporting require the accumulation of data and can be handled at some point in the future.

Although the procedures used for assessing outcome may vary, outcome assessment need not be painful to the clinician or client. In fact, it can be quite painless and informative for everyone involved if the proper measure is chosen, the proper procedure is followed, and the data are used in an efficient and helpful way. Within the next chapter we consider this last point, using the data to inform practice for the individual client.

🖋 TEST YOURSELF 🖋

1. **When is the best time to administer an outcome instrument for a new client who is coming to an intake appointment?**

   (a) Immediately after the session

   (b) Via telephone survey after the client returns home

   (c) Immediately before the session

   (d) During the session

   (e) None of the above

2. **Which of the following is *not* a drawback of retrospective (survey) data gathering for outcome assessment?**

   (a) High attrition rates

   (b) Not helpful for that particular patient

   (c) High cost

   (d) No comparison of pre- and posttreatment change

   (e) Low survey response rates

3. **Which of the following is a reason that prospective data is preferred over retrospective data?**

   (a) Lower cost

   (b) Provides feedback for the client and therapist

   (c) Requires less effort on the part of clinicians

   (d) Requires only one data point

   (e) All of the above

4. **Which of the following is the most important reason for avoiding pre- versus posttherapy outcome assessment only in favor of multiple time periods of assessment?**

   (a) The data in pre-post assessments are not available for the clinicians and client to modify treatment.

   (b) Clinicians vary in their opinions of when treatment actually should end for clients.

   (c) Pretreatment assessments tend to utilize idiographic data only.

   (d) Survey response rates tend to be low.

   (e) None of the above.

5. How often was it recommended that outcome data be collected?

(a) At intake and then every sixth session thereafter

(b) Pre-post only

(c) At intake and then every six months thereafter

(d) At intake and then every session thereafter

(e) Every three months

6. Which of the following individuals would be most likely to gather follow-up data?

(a) A clinician at a community mental health center

(b) A clinical researcher at a behavioral therapy laboratory

(c) A clinician at an outpatient child treatment center

(d) A registered nurse at a community mental health center

(e) All of the above

7. Which of the following individuals should ideally collect outcome assessment data?

(a) Clerical staff.

(b) Therapist.

(c) Neither; it should be done by telephone survey.

(d) Neither; it should be done by mail survey.

(e) It does not matter who collects the data as long as it is collected.

8. Outcome assessment instruments with computerized scannable entry forms

(a) should not be used due to the inherent problems that exist with them.

(b) should be used sparingly because they do not provide individualized data.

(c) should be used more frequently because they are cheaper.

(d) should not be used due to a lack of validity.

(e) should be used with discretion after being inspected for data entry errors or stray marks.

Answers: 1. c; 2. c; 3. b; 4. a; 5. d; 6. b; 7. a; 8. e

Four

USING OUTCOME DATA TO INFORM PRACTICE

After the clinician has selected measures for the assessment of outcome and developed routine procedures for gathering outcome assessment data, methods for using the data within the clinical setting must be implemented. In reality, the outcome data may or may not be used by the clinician. Many agency evaluation procedures run parallel to the typical clinical processes and the clinicians only have access to the data months or years later when the data show up in agency reports or published articles; this raises the need to distinguish between measuring, monitoring, and managing outcomes (see Rapid Reference 4.1).

Measuring outcome refers to the use of outcome assessment instruments to gauge the degree to which clients change during treatment. Measurement of outcome, however, may occur independent of any clinical use of the data. An agency evaluator could gather outcome data without clinicians' even knowing that the data are being collected. The data could then be aggregated to create internal reports, evaluate programs, or generate published research. Monitoring outcome implies something more than mere measurement. To monitor or track outcome, the clinician has access to the outcome data as feedback regarding client progress. The clinician can see whether the client is making expected improvements and benefiting from treatment. Finally, managing outcome extends the use of the data one level further and includes the potential modification of treatment based on the measurement and monitoring of outcome. The management of outcome implies (but does not necessitate) the potential inclusion of a third party who is not involved in treatment (e.g., supervisor, managed-care case worker). This person may monitor progress and then make recommendations regarding the modification of the treatment plan based on the client's progress. The managers may also be the clinicians—that is, they monitor and modify treatment themselves. In some cases, the manager of a case may be the payor. Based on client progress, the case manager may make decisions regarding the number of sessions to pay for, when to include specialty care (e.g., hospitalization), and other issues.

≣Rapid Reference 4.1

Measuring outcome means using outcome instruments to assess the outcome of treatment.

Monitoring outcome means using outcome assessment data during treatment to track client progress.

Managing outcome means using outcome monitoring data to modify treatment as necessary.

Mental health professionals are more frequently being challenged by administrators, insurance companies, and other third-party payors to demonstrate that services provided have had a positive effect on client functioning or well-being in an increasingly challenging environment (Plante, Couchman, & Hoffman, 1998). Specifically, the managed-care movement in the 1980s has been a springboard for outcome assessment and accountability for agencies that provide mental health services (Lambert, 2001). Although the possibility of outsiders' managing care through the use of outcome data is potentially threatening to practitioners, it is not necessarily uninformed or exclusively focused on managing costs. Using outcome data to aid in the assurance of quality care is a legitimate and potentially appropriate purpose if carried out in a helpful manner.

Aside from the challenges of outside sources such as insurance companies and legislative bodies, Andrews (1995) has taken the position that outcome assessment is a phenomenon that extends beyond the push from specific payment systems. Indeed, outcome assessment, because it has the potential to benefit the mental health consumer, may be just another step toward providing quality mental healthcare worldwide to clients in need. Whether by choice or by persuasion from outside parties, mental health professionals are finding themselves more involved in outcome assess-

DON'T FORGET

....

Of all the decisions regarding outcome assessment and assessment instruments, the most important is how to use the data after they are obtained.

ment. They may use it to their benefit even if not paid through a managed-care entity.

Because there is no sidestepping the importance of outcome assessment, clinicians can focus on making the assessment more useful for informing practice. A special section in the *Journal of Consulting and Clinical Psychology* (Lambert, 2001) was devoted to this very topic as it pertains to patient-focused research. Thus, the question for clinicians has shifted from *should we do outcome assessment* to *how can we best inform clinical practice with outcome assessment?* Indeed, the most important part of implementing an outcome assessment protocol is determining how best to use the information that is obtained in the assessment (Smith, Fischer, Nordquist, Mosley, & Ledbetter, 1997).

To illustrate the importance of utilizing outcome assessment information to inform practice, consider the example of a college history course examination. Students enrolled in a college history class are supposed to learn material that is deemed important, such as historical facts, important dates, and the names of historical figures. Imagine the surprise and bewilderment of the students (and college administrators) if they were informed that the instructor planned to not have tests, research papers, or any other formal, quantified manner of assessment. Instead, the instructor planned to decide at some point when the class had learned enough, and the instructor would gauge student learning or retention of key facts through everyday interactions in the class. Although these are not ideal conditions, one could argue that the class members in this situation could learn about history just the same. However, there would be no way of knowing that the students had mastered some of the important concepts in the course unless they were assessed in some way. Furthermore, without some method of assessment, the class meetings might lack both structure and focus because it would be difficult to plan for what would come next in the class. Indeed, the tests or research papers in a history class might serve a function as a sort of road map for students and the instructor to help both understand and gauge where they have been and where they are going next in the course. Thus, student progress in the class is measured, monitored, and managed better when there is some sort of formal assessment.

Just like the test in the history class, outcome assessment serves a similar function in behavioral health treatment. When implementing outcome assessment processes in an outpatient practice, the data can be used to measure, monitor, or manage the cases. Each clinician and agency will need to make the decision regarding the most practical method of using the data. The data can be used to inform the initial assessment (including treatment planning and decisions about anticipated intensity and length of treatment), monitor or track treatment progress, and modifying treatment based on current client progress. In short, this chapter focuses more on taking the knowledge obtained from outcome assessment, regardless of the instruments used or time at which they are completed, and using that data to better inform practice with the individual client.

> **DON'T FORGET**
>
> Although the initial administration of an outcome measure is meant to be the baseline for future assessment of progress, the outcome measure can also give the clinician information that will be useful for intake assessment and treatment planning.

INITIAL ASSESSMENT

Although the primary purpose of giving an outcome instrument at intake is to gather baseline data from which to compare future administrations of the instrument, the data are also useful for the initial assessment. When an outcome measure is administered prior to the first session, the measure can be used for treatment planning and initial assessment. The outcome measure is not likely to provide the detailed information that can be obtained through a complete diagnostic assessment or the administration of other more lengthy psychological measures that are specifically designed for personality assessment. The initial administration of an outcome measure, however, can provide information regarding the client's initial level of severity, critical needs, target areas for focus, and

DON'T FORGET

Outcome assessment devices can provide information regarding the initial level of severity, immediate needs, and central complaints and strengths.

client strengths. We now highlight why this information is important in outcome assessment.

Overall Severity

Client initial level of severity data refer to how well the client is doing based on the quantitative data generated by the outcome instrument. Overall ratings of initial severity can be compared to normative data on the instrument to assess the client's level of distress in relationship to other client groups (e.g., inpatient samples, outpatient samples, community samples). Most instruments provide a normative comparison group that allows the clinician to assess whether the overall level of severity falls in the clinical range. In addition, some instruments provide ranges of scores that indicate whether the client's overall distress falls in the mild, moderate, or severe range. As a result, the initial total score can give the clinician some idea about the overall distress of the client.

Importantly, initial level of severity may be predictive of the needed intensity or duration of treatment. As a result, the type of treatment the client receives may be based in part on pretreatment scores on the outcome measure. If clients have a mild level of overall distress, they may be referred to brief therapy. Clients who register extremely high scores may need services in addition to outpatient treatment such as hospitalization, day treatment, pharmacotherapy, or a host of other treatment options. Some administrators may wish to devise cutoff scores on outcome scales that indicate consideration of certain types of treatment (i.e., level of care) the client might need. For example, a score of 70 or greater on a particular scale might indicate biweekly therapy as opposed to weekly treatment. Although this is not a bad idea, other information should also be utilized when making treatment decisions of this nature. Recall that a single measure from a single informant may not be reliable. Particularly with children there are sometimes discrepancies in the severity of pathology based on information obtained from different informants. In short, the outcome assessment may provide useful initial information regarding level of care, but it should not be used independent of other sources of clinical data.

> # CAUTION
>
> Outcome assessment devices can provide useful information at intake, but they should not be used for decision making independent of other clinical data.

As we will see later, expected improvement curves are also related to initial severity. Similarly, initial severity rates can be very important in determining which patients may respond poorly to mental health interventions (Meier & Letsch, 2000). As data are gathered regarding all clients entering services, more useful protocols and predictions may be available for clinicians to use in determining the type and intensity of services.

In addition to information regarding the overall severity of distress, outcome measures may be examined at the item level to provide individualized, or idiographic, information. This information may be useful for identifying critical areas of need, targeting concerns and strengths, and developing a treatment plan.

Critical Needs

Critical items are those items on any outcome measure that would draw clinical attention if they were endorsed by the client, regardless of the overall problem severity score. Items that assess suicidal ideation, homicidal ideation, drug usage, lawbreaking behaviors, and other areas of key concern would represent critical items on the typical outcome measure. In some computer-scored versions of measures, the critical items endorsed by clients are highlighted to call the clinician's attention to that particular item. Even if they are not highlighted in a report, the clinician can examine directly specified items immediately (prior to the session) when retrieving the completed instrument. It is extremely important that clinicians pay attention to the critical items, because they often are related to issues of personal safety for the client, the client's family, or others in the client's environment. Even if a client has no significant scores on an overall measure or

> **DON'T FORGET**
> ....
> Selected items on outcome mea-
> sures can be examined to identify
> critical needs (i.e., safety concerns)
> and target problems for initial as-
> sessment and treatment planning.

outcome subscale, elevated critical items may warrant clinical attention and treatment in their own right. Investigating client endorsement of critical items can also be helpful in formulating a treatment plan. For example, clients who endorse an item related to suicidal ideation will need more frequent assessment of current thoughts, closer monitoring regarding session-to-session mood, and appropriate interventions.

Treatment Targets

Examining client item-level responses on the outcome instrument may also identify client target or central complaints. Many public mental health service guidelines require the establishment of a treatment plan for each client. The treatment plan may require the identification of clear treatment goals or target problems and associated methods of intervention and expected outcomes. By examining the items, the clinician may identify key target problems that can be used on the treatment plan. Examining the ratings on those items over time may also serve as the established outcome for the target. For example, a client with a total score in the moderate range may endorse a cluster of items related to depression at the high end of the item-scale (e.g., 4 or 5 on a 5-point scale). The clinician can note these particular items as potential targets for treatment, discuss them with the client during the initial interview, and potentially use the selected items as individualized measures of change.

By discussing the items that are endorsed as most severe with the client, the clinician acknowledges the client's effort in completing the measure and may help to establish a stronger therapeutic relationship. After all, it is ultimately the client's treatment and it is important that clients have an active voice in the creation of a treatment plan (Dorwart et al., 1996). As the clinician communicates an interest in helping resolve what the client believes to be the biggest problems, then that individual is probably more likely to view the relationship as both important and collaborative in nature. In addition, the client will be more likely to see the importance of completing the outcome measure over time, particularly if it is completed numerous times throughout treatment.

Another way to gauge target complaints is through direct communication with clients about their most serious problems. During the typical initial assessment, clients should be asked to describe in their own words the two or three problems that they would most like to see change over the course of treatment. The items on the outcome measure may provide this same information, yet asking directly about the problems adds some minimal standardization in the rating of the problems over time. Of course, there will be occasions when the client's central problems are not included within the outcome measure. In those cases, the outcome measure can still be used for other purposes described in this chapter.

Personal Strengths: The Hidden Facilitator

Clinicians, for better or worse, are often trained to focus on pathology in behavioral health clients. Similarly, most psychological assessment instruments are interpreted in the context of what maladaptive traits or characteristics are keeping a person from being psychologically healthy, or what deficiencies are keeping people from functioning well in society. Although it is certainly informative and useful to investigate problem areas for clients through outcome measures, it is equally important to focus on strengths that the client displays (see Rapid Reference 4.2). Because it is often not the focus of clinical attention, personal strengths can be referred to as the hidden facilitator in treat-

≡Rapid Reference 4.2

Client strengths are sometimes overlooked in an initial assessment, but can be valuable in formulating and supporting the treatment plan. Some outcome measures provide information regarding client strengths at the initial assessment. An examination of selected items may identify potential strengths for incorporation into treatment.

ment. Although often overlooked, some outcome measures may provide information regarding functional strengths for clients. These strengths can be useful in formulating a treatment plan and facilitating client improvement. For example, the Outcome Questionnaire includes several items that could be examined to identify potential client strengths, including *I get along well with others, I feel loved and wanted, I feel my love relationships are full and complete,* and *I am satisfied with my life.* If a client responds favorably to any or all of these items, the clinician has access to some obvious potential client strengths. These strengths can be followed up with further discussion and potentially incorporated into the treatment plan. In some public services, the identification of client strengths is a mandated part of initial assessment. As a result, the use of the outcome measure in this way facilitates the required clinical assessment.

Initial Assessment: Summary

Through an examination of the total score and individual items, the initial administration of the outcome measure prior to treatment may provide useful information. We included four specific methods of using the data: assessing the initial severity of the case, identifying critical needs through an examination of critical items, identifying potential targets of treatment through locating the items that are rated as the most severe, and identifying potential strengths through examination of selected items. Although the information from outcome measures at intake is useful, the central purpose of routine outcome assessment remains the measurement of change.

TRACKING SESSION-BY-SESSION CHANGE

A number of writers address the use of outcome measures to track or monitor individual change. For example, Howard, Moras, Brill, Martinovich, and Lutz (1996) describe the benefits of gathering individual patient outcome data. They refer to this method as patient-focused research. This type of research has the goal of improving patient outcome on an individual level. Rather than focusing on the empirical history of treatment approaches for *groups* of clients, clinicians using patient-focused data can make changes in treatment based on current findings from outcome data on the individual client. The information gathered during treatment and utilized in treatment planning represents a so-called bottom-up approach to treatment and outcome assessment (Lambert, 2001).

Session-by-session change research on the individual client can be either qualitative or quantitative in nature (Roth & Fonagy, 1996). In a case in which baseline measures for an individual are noted and adequate controls exist throughout treatment, the patient's outcome may be studied in a quantitative manner with prior performance serving as his or her control group. Each patient can serve as a single-case study for the clinician to evaluate (Roth & Fonagy, 1996). Of course, the results of session-by-session outcome assessments are valid only for that client and cannot be generalized to other client groups. However, the advantage of gathering this type of data is that the results are more relevant for the specific patient than are group-based findings.

The primary way that change is tracked from session to session is a simple comparison of the client's progress from session one to session two to session three, and so on. Clinicians monitor client scores on an outcome measure, noting whether a client continually worsens or improves after one or several sessions. For example, let's consider a fictional patient who was participating in treatment for depression. The client was moderately impaired at the beginning of treatment and originally scored a 32 on the Beck Depression Inventory (BDI). Since that time, the patient has progressively scored higher and higher to the point that by the fourth session she has a score of 52 on the same measure. This increase indicates a worsening of symptoms (higher scores mean more impairment) and may indicate the need for modifications in treatment. Perhaps the client needs to be seen more frequently, or the possibility of antidepressant medication should be considered, or perhaps the sessions need to be focused on other topics, or maybe she has suffered a setback in her personal life. At any rate, the worsening of symptoms after beginning treatment warrants clinician consideration of potential causes and potential courses of action. The increase in the scores thus serves as valuable feedback for the clinician and ultimately for the client if the information is used to improve treatment.

In contrast, let's consider an example that is the opposite of that just proposed. Imagine that another client has begun treatment and completed an initial assessment on the same measure scoring a 32. After 8 weeks/sessions of treatment, this client's scores on the BDI have decreased to a score of 11. This too is valuable information for the clinician. The improvement, although not necessarily due only to therapy, may indicate that treatment is helping. Another hypothesis is that the client has improved greatly and that services could now be titrated a bit, perhaps from one session per week to one every month. Again, the specific details of what to do with the information are up to the clinician and ultimately the client. However, the outcome data is one source of standardized information that is important and can be beneficial to future treatment.

The actual mechanics of tracking change can be facilitated by standard reports that are generated electronically via entering the outcome data into a database each session or by hand scoring and tracking using graphs. For example, Figure 4.1 displays a graph that is included in the Ohio Scales manual. The graph is available for the clinician to chart the total scores at each data collection point over time. The graph can then be examined to track the direction of client change. Notice that the lines below the horizontal axis include a place for the parent, youth, and agency worker score and the date. Since this instrument has forms for multiple parallel sources, the progress on all three forms can be charted on the same graph. In most cases, however, the client data alone will be charted at each session. Virtually any global, client-rated outcome measure can be used to track session-by-session progress in this fashion.

Clinical Significance

While a client may be making steady improvement, the natural question that arises is how much improvement is enough. In our previous examples, the differences in the scores were so large that they would most certainly have been meaningful from a clinical standpoint. However, clinicians

Tracking Problem Severity

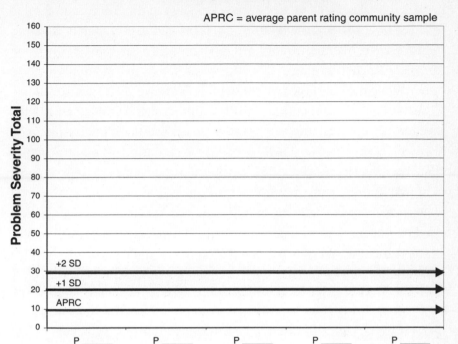

Figure 4.1 Tracking Form Ohio Scales Problem Severity

Note: P = parent rating, Y = child rating, W = agency worker rating.

would be better served to evaluate changes in outcome scores using a standard method of determining the amount of change that is necessary to be considered meaningful (Ogles, Lunnen, & Bonesteel, 2001).

To understand current methods of identifying meaningful change, a brief excursion into the literature regarding clinically significant change is necessary. Statistically significant change refers to changes in scores that are deemed significant by a statistical test. One way that statistically significant change in therapy has been demonstrated is through the comparison of groups of patients, in which one group received treatment and another group either received no treatment or an alternative treatment. Mean scores on various scales would then be compared between the groups, and the differences would be evaluated statistically. If the treatment group made more improvements than the control group (statistically determined), then the treatment is said to be effective, or efficacious. This is the traditional method of evaluating the benefits of psychotherapy (Lambert & Bergin, 1994).

Tests of statistical significance, although they can be informative, have their limitations. First, they are not particularly useful for the treatment of a specific client (Barlow, 1981). Second, the results are often difficult for clinicians to interpret (Lick, 1973). Clinical significance, by way of comparison, has to do with the amount of change that is necessary for the individual client to be considered improved, recovered, or meaningfully better. The operative word in the previous sentence is *meaningfully*, because statistically significant change is not necessarily meaningful or clinically significant change.

In the current behavioral health care market, consumers of outcome data want evidence that clients benefit from treatment. The statistical tests that researchers offer, however, do not always provide the most relevant information. Statistical tests may also be difficult for many outcome consumers to understand. In addition, statistical tests do not provide information regarding the effectiveness of treatment for any one individual. As a result, methods for determining and displaying the clinical meaningfulness of client change may facilitate the description and dissemination of outcome data in practice. These methods have been developed in the psychotherapy research literature and are helpful to the clinician who wants to determine when a client has made meaningful change.

Jacobson and colleagues (Jacobson, Follete, & Revenstorf, 1984; Jacobson, Roberts, Berns, & McGlinchey, 1999; Jacobson & Truax, 1991) proposed a standardized method for determining clinical significance. This method is based on the assumption that clinically significant change involves a return to normal functioning. Jacobson and Truax (1991) propose two criteria for assessing clinical significance: (a) Clients should move from the dysfunctional range to the functional range on a measure of change as a result of treatment. For example, a youth receiving outpatient therapy should have a global severity score after treatment that is more similar to the scores for the general population of youth than to other clinical samples of youth, and (b) the pre- to posttreatment change must be large enough so that differences can be attributed to real change and not to random or systematic measurement error—said another way, the change must be reliable. Jacobson and Truax (1991) provide a method to calculate a Reliable Change Index (RCI). The change is considered reliable if the change index is greater than 1.96. If the client meets both criteria, movement to the functional range and an RCI greater than 1.96, then the change is considered *clinically significant*. When a client has the fortune to reach this plateau, this end of treatment status is also sometimes labeled *recovered*.

A number of other issues must be considered when using the Jacobson method, but a thorough discussion of the difficulties and issues is beyond the scope of this book. Interested readers can refer to other sources for a more detailed review (e.g., Kendall, Marrs-Garcia, Nath, & Sheldrick, 1999; Kendall & Grove, 1988; Ogles, Lambert, & Masters, 1996; Ogles, Lunnen, & Bonesteel, 2001; Tingey, Lambert, Burlingame, & Hansen, 1999). Using the Jacobson method and data regarding various samples published in test manuals, one can identify cutoff and change scores that are necessary for calculating meaningful change. Table 4.1 presents the cutoff scores and

Table 4.1 Clinical Significance Data for Several Scales

Scale	Reliable Change Index	Cutoff
OQ (total score)	14	64
SCL-90-R (GSI raw score)	.32	.62
Ohio Scales—parent-rated problem severity	10	25
CBCL (total problem)	9	42
BDI	9	13
Fear Questionnaire	7	11
Dyadic Adjustment Scale	9	97

change scores for several of the global scales included in Chapter 2. The numbers produced in the table are based on other manuals for the instruments and other samples described in the literature (Ogles, Lambert, & Masters, 1996). Site-specific norms may sometimes be more useful than the norms provided in the table.

To use the data produced in Table 4.1, the clinician takes the client's pretreatment score and last measurement point score and calculates the amount of change. For example, if the client's raw score on the Global Severity Scale of the SCL-90-R decreased by .32 points, then it would be considered a reliable change (improvement). In addition, the last treatment score is compared to the cutoff (on the SCL-90-R, did the raw score fall below .93). If both criteria are met, then the client could be said to have made clinically meaningful change (recovery). Some other examples of client-by-client determinations of meaningful change are displayed in Table 4.2.

Now, we move on to the use of this information while tracking change.

Table 4.2 Examples of Individual Scores That Result in Categorization as Improved, Recovered, No Change, or Deteriorated

Instrument	Intake Score	Last Session Score	Amount of Change	Classification
BDI	22	8	14	Recovered
BDI	22	14	8	No change
BDI	22	25	–3	No change
OQ-45	80	58	22	Recovered
OQ-45	80	64	16	Improved
OQ-45	100	75	25	Improved
FQ	16	25	–99	Deteriorated
FQ	15	21	–6	No change
FQ	22	14	8	Improved
FQ	21	7	14	Recovered

When the clinician is tracking change using a graph or automatic report, predefined amounts of change and cutoffs can be used to identify when clients make meaningful improvement. This information can then be used by the clinician to decide when clients have meaningfully improved. The clinician can also use the clinical significance methodology to describe the change in clinical reports or for external reporting in this way: "John Doe entered treatment with an OQ-45 score of 75. This is typical of clients who receive outpatient psychotherapy and indicates a mild to moderate level of initial distress. After 3 months and 12 sessions of outpatient service, John had an OQ-45 score of 42. This end-of-treatment score is similar to that of nondistressed individuals living in the community (within 1 standard deviation of the community sample mean). The magnitude or size of change (33 points) also indicates that he made a reliable change for the better."

Graphic Depiction by Group

A final method of utilizing the Jacobson method involves the graphic depiction of pre- to posttreatment change for individuals or groups of individuals. For example, Figure 4.2 displays a graph with the parent-rated problem severity on the Ohio Scales at intake on the bottom of the graph and the posttreatment score on the left side of the graph. The horizontal line (posttreatment score = 25) represents the cutoff score necessary to be considered part of the functional group following treatment. The diagonal line running from corner to corner is the *line of no change*. Clients who have the same pretreatment and posttreatment total will be plotted on this line (Client A). The dashed diagonal lines on either side of the line of no change represent the change scores necessary to result in an RCI greater than 1.96. Clients between the dashed diagonal lines (Client B) did not improve sufficiently to rule out random fluctuations or test unreliability as the source of the change (RCI < 1.96). Clients plotted outside the lines (above the top line or below the bottom line) can be considered to have made reliable changes (RCI > 1.96). For example, Client C made changes for the better (below the bottom line) and Client D made changes for the worse (above the top line). Individuals who made reliable improvement and had end-of-

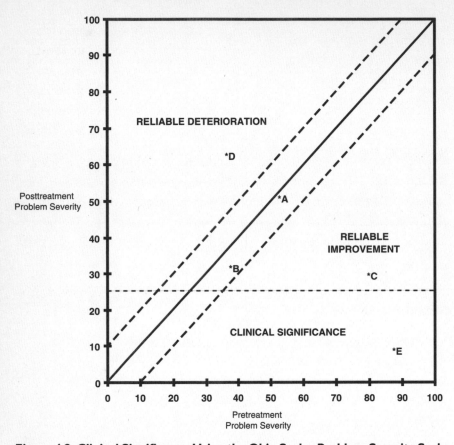

Figure 4.2 Clinical Significance Using the Ohio Scales Problem Severity Scale

Source: Reprinted from Ogles, B. M., Lunnen, K. M., & Bonesteel, K. (2001). Clinical significance: History, application, and current practice. Copyright 2001 by Elsevier Science. Reprinted with permission.

treatment scores similar to those of the healthy population are plotted below the diagonal and the cutoff score (Client E).

Clinicians can develop and use similar figures with any instrument—several pre-made figures are available in Ogles, Lambert, and Masters (1996). The clinician can easily draw the figures by putting the range of scores for the outcome measure on both the vertical and horizontal axes. A diagonal line is then added that represents no change (e.g., 50 before treatment and 50 at the last measurement point). The bands around the diagonal are determined by the number of points required to make a reliable change; these bands vary depending on the instrument. They can be obtained from the table or calculated by the clinician using data produced in the manual that is provided with each instrument. The figures are also useful for plotting groups of clients (e.g., similar diagnosis, same program) to ascertain the proportion of clients who make clinically meaningful changes. Finally, the principles described here regarding the determination of meaningful treatment surface in many of the examples presented later in this chapter and in our discussion of aggregate change in Chapter 5.

Individualized Change

As mentioned previously, it may also be useful to selectively track specific problem areas that were identified for clinical work. In this case, the clinician tracks change on predetermined items. For example, consider a client who rates the following three items on the CORE as a 4 (*most of the time*) at intake—*I have felt unhappy, I have felt despairing or hopeless,* and *I have been unable to do most things I needed to.* The clinician can examine the client's responses to these three items for evidence of improvement in an individualized manner. Such an analysis can supplement the examination of the total score changes over time. Although this method is not as flexible as the target complaints or goal attainment scaling approach described in Chapter 2 (because it is limited by the items on the instrument), it is similar to that approach and allows some variation or individualization among clients (different items are used for different clients). Another advantage of this method is that it does not require the administration of two scales.

Summary

Three methods of tracking change may be useful for the clinician. First, the clinician can track client change on a global score using hand charts or automated reports to examine the client's progress over time. Second, the amount of client change can be examined in order to determine when the client has made meaningful improvement (or deterioration). Third, individual items can be examined over time to find evidence of change on specific targets of treatment.

To this point we have considered the monitoring of change with only allusions to the management of change. Although we have suggested that tracking change will inform the potential modification of treatment, we have presented relatively little information regarding specific potential uses of the data for modification. In the next section we consider one specific application of outcome monitoring that extends into outcome management—the use of data to enhance the outcome for failing patients.

USING DATA ON TYPICAL TREATMENT RESPONSE TO ENHANCE THE OUTCOME OF THERAPY

After monitoring data are available to review client progress, decision rules can be developed using tools such as the clinical significance formulas to trigger the modification or review of ongoing treatment. The continually growing patient-oriented research literature provides the fundamental data necessary for comparing various client improvement rates. Not only can the amount of change necessary for the change to be considered meaningful be determined, but aggregate data from individuals with similar profiles also can be used to calculate expected rates of improvement for a specific client. Although this method is not foolproof, research in this area can help to establish models for expected rate of improvement, decline, or even dropout from mental health treatment. Expected rates of improvement can be especially helpful to clinicians in situations in which they are treating patients who may not be improving. The next section addresses methods for identifying clients who are not improving as expected. The actual changes in interventions must be determined by the clinician. As a result, we focus on the use of the data for identifying failing cases using expected patterns of improvement.

Although a majority (40 to 70%) of clients who undergo a course of psychotherapy have a positive outcome, a significant minority of clients either fail to improve or actually deteriorate (10%) while in treatment (Lambert & Bergin, 1994; Mohr, 1995; Smith, Glass, & Miller, 1980). This fact

combined with the advent of managed-care organizations has led to
the development of quality management efforts aimed at improving the quality of behavioral health
services. Often case-management
procedures within these organizations are intended to identify and

> **DON'T FORGET**
>
> Around 40 to 70% of patients who enter therapy have a positive outcome, but about 10% of patients who enter therapy leave treatment worse off than when they started.

monitor the failing patient and to enhance the likelihood of a positive outcome (Lambert, Heufner, & Reisinger, 2000).

Recent developments in quality management for psychotherapy favor the continuous monitoring of patient treatment response to determine whether a treatment is adequate for a particular patient (Kordy, Hannöver, & Richard, 2001; Lambert, Hansen, & Finch, 2001; Leuger et al., 2001). Clinicians routinely but informally monitor treatment progress, making adjustments in their behavior in accordance with theoretical considerations, the needs and characteristics of their patients, and the patients' responses to treatment; yet the therapist's ability to make accurate prognostic assessments even late in therapy has been called into question (Breslin, Sobell, Buchan, & Cunningham, 1997; Meyer & Schulte, in press) especially with patients who show deterioration (Lambert & Bergin, 1994; Lunnen & Ogles, 1998). Decision enhancement tools offer the possibility of assisting the clinician's attempt to identify clients whose progress is in doubt. In light of this information, a *stepped-care* approach, in which the failing patient is stepped up or down to more or less intensive treatment, may be indicated.

Decision support tools based on decision-analytic concepts and techniques are being used in various branches of medicine, particularly those in which clinical judgment is involved in the interpretation of nonbiological, cognitive-perceptual data, to standardize and improve quality. In psychotherapy, quality management efforts can be informed by research on patterns of change over the course of therapy and evidence that early response to therapy predicts final outcome. For example, Richard and Kordy (in press) found four distinct patterns of change in the course of treatment for patients with bulimia, two suggesting a positive final outcome and two suggesting treatment failure. The patterns were recognizable by the fourth week of treatment. Tang and DeRubies (1999a, 1999b) found that rapid improvement in depressive symptoms foretold better ultimate outcome and follow-up functioning than did slow improvement. Haas et al. (in press) reported the same finding in patients with a variety of disorders treated with a variety of theoretically based treatments. Wilson (1999), commenting on early response to treatment, suggested the clear practical consequence of early poor response and the possibility of modifying treatment prior to termination for these patients. Research in this area appears to suggest that patterns of treatment response can lead to early identification of particular clients who are in need of special treatment efforts.

Using large data sets of repeated measures of individual patient progress, Brown and Lambert (1998) found that a client's initial level of severity combined with change after one session of therapy predicted final outcome (R^2 = .17). Furthermore, initial level of severity plus change from pretreatment through session three was an even better predictor, accounting for 40% of the variance in final outcome status (see Rapid Reference 4.3). In general, more disturbed clients required more therapy sessions to meet criteria of recovery (as defined via Jacobson's clinical significance method described above). This information, in combination with the desire to set up decision support tools for the clinician and case manager, resulted in the development of a rationally derived method of identifying cases for review and management; this was later followed by an empirically derived method for identifying failing cases.

Both methods are suitable for use in clinical practice. Because they can be readily applied in clinical settings, the rationally and empirically derived methods of identifying cases for review in therapy are fine examples of how outcome

═Rapid Reference 4.3

The best predictors of final outcome are initial level of disturbance and initial treatment response. Those patients who show fast substantial progress are likely to show a positive treatment outcome at termination and maintenance of treatment effects at follow-up. Early substantial negative change is a good predictor of deterioration at termination and at follow-up.

assessment can be used to go beyond the monitoring of treatment and move toward the management of clinical practice. A brief description of the methodology used to arrive at each method is provided in the following paragraphs.

The Rationally Derived Method

Information about early response to treatment, the dose-response relationship, and clinically significant change were used (Lambert et al., 2001) to create algorithms for identifying clients who were predicted to leave treatment before receiving therapeutic benefit or who were thought to be at risk for having a negative treatment outcome. For simplicity of communication in the clinical setting, those so identified were referred to as *signal-alarm cases;* this is a term that has precedence in other research aimed at improving the quality of patient care (Kordy, Hannöver, & Richard, 2001). A matrix was created for identification of signal-alarm cases. The vertical axis was used to plot intake OQ-45 scores across the possible range of scores from 0 to 180. The horizontal axis was used to plot *change* (change from intake to a given session) scores at the sessions of interest. An example matrix is displayed in Figure 4.3.

It proved difficult to make decisions about satisfactory patient progress for every session that a patient could receive; also, such a procedure would necessitate 20 or more separate matrices, each dealing with the effects of that session and one varying only slightly from the next. Therefore, it was decided to lump sessions into groupings, creating three matrices. These matrices grouped treatment sessions 2 through 4, 5 through 9, and 10 and above. The reasoning used to create three matrices was that insufficient change after two to four sessions of treatment would not be as alarming as the same insufficient progress after five to nine (or more) sessions of treatment.

> **DON'T FORGET**
> ....
> Signal-alarm cases are those individuals who are predicted to leave treatment before receiving therapeutic benefit or who are thought to be at risk for having a negative treatment outcome.

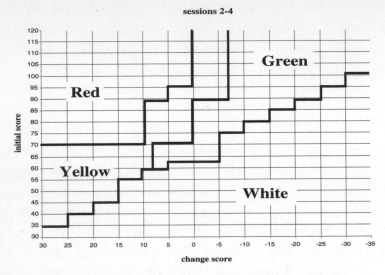

Figure 4.3 Example Feedback Algorithm Chart Using the OQ-45

Source: Reprinted by permission of M. J. Lambert.

The expert judges began to imagine specific scenarios with the intent of classifying specific patients into four classifications based on colored signals. The yellow category signified that the patient's progress might be insufficient and the therapist needed to be cautioned about possible treatment failure. The red category signified more serious concern and the need to signal the therapist to seriously reconsider the ongoing treatment regimen. The green category signified that a patient had made significant progress during their course of treatment. A white category was used to alert the therapist to the fact that the patient's functioning (OQ-45 score) was within the normal range.

After scenarios for sessions 2 through 4 were created, the same procedures were repeated for the imagined patient who had had 5 through 9 sessions of treatment. And the same procedures were again done for patients who had 10 or more sessions of treatment. The two raters would imagine patients who started at a specific OQ-45 score, then imagine the patients worsening by 1 point, 2 points, 3 points, and so on. At a given point, depending on the patients' intake scores, a degree of worsening would become large enough that the raters would reach a consensus that a yellow signal was warranted, and then a red signal. As noted previously, movement in a positive direction was given a white categorization when the patients' change score put them in the functional range (e.g., at or below a score of 63 on the OQ-45).

Some examples of the procedures can help clarify the way cutoff points were devised. A client could be imagined who began treatment with an OQ-45 score of 75. This score is an average score for patients entering treatment in outpatient clinics and about 1½ standard deviations above the mean of nonpatients. The raters considered the patient's worsening after having two to four sessions of treatment, 1 point, 2 points, 3 points, and so on, and agreed that if the patient had made a negative change of 1 point (after this dosage of therapy), a yellow warning was appropriate, and that getting worse by 9 points (about two thirds of the RCI of 14 points) would qualify him or her for a red warning.

In contrast to this patient, consider a patient who enters treatment with a score of 95 (a score that is close to the mean of inpatients, about 1 standard deviation above outpatients, and 2 standard deviations above nonpatients). This score suggests severe distress and a need for relief. The expert judges agreed that an improvement of less than 7 points after two to four sessions of treatment should signal a yellow caution, and no change or any worsening at all should result in a red signal. A white signal categorization was given if the patient changed by 32 points or more (indicating their score at the session of interest had moved to 63 or below). Otherwise a green signal was considered appropriate.

Similar decisions were made to form the matrices for sessions 5 to 9 and for 10 and above. The rules for classification for these matrices were based on the meaning of changing or not changing after this higher dosage of treatment. For example, the situation of a patient who starts treatment with a score of 70 on the OQ-45 and does not change after two treatment sessions was not considered to be as alarming, so to speak, as this patient's failure to change after nine treatment sessions.

After a patient takes the OQ-45, commences treatment, and completes two sessions of treatment, the decision rules can be used to generate feedback in the form of a progress graph and a colored dot. In the original studies of feedback using this method, colored red, yellow, white, and green ¼-in. paste-on dots were used to visually catch the therapist's attention and immediately convey the status of patient progress. A graph of patient progress and a dot were given to the therapist each time a subsequent OQ-45 was administered.

A graphic presentation of this matrix (e.g., decision rules) for sessions 2 through 4 is presented in Figure 4.3. The vertical axis represents a patient's initial score, and the horizontal axis depicts the change following two to four sessions of therapy (separate graphs for later sessions present slightly different predictions). For example, if the patient started with a score of 75 (vertical axis) and after three sessions improved by −3 (horizontal axis) the therapist would be given a green dot. A patient who started therapy with an OQ-45 score of 60 and worsened by +25 points (therefore scoring 85 at the session of interest) would receive a yellow dot. There were four possible feedback codes: white, green, yellow, and red. The area within the matrix (see Figure 4.3) indicates which feedback message would be delivered to the therapist:

- **White feedback:** The client is functioning in the normal range. Consider termination.
- **Green feedback:** The rate of change the client is making is in the adequate range. No change in the treatment plan is recommended.
- **Yellow feedback:** The rate of change the client is making is less than adequate. Consider altering the treatment plan by intensifying treatment, shifting intervention strategies, and monitoring progress especially carefully. This client may end up with no significant benefit from therapy.
- **Red feedback:** The client is not making the expected level of progress. Chances are he or she may drop out of treatment prematurely or have a negative treatment outcome. Steps should be taken to review this case carefully and decide upon a new course of action such as referral for medication or intensification of treatment. The treatment plan should be reconsidered. Consider-

ation should also be given to presenting this client at case conference. The client's readiness for change may need to be reassessed.

These algorithms can result in feedback for a clinician after each administration of the instrument. As previously noted, the algorithms use two data points: The client's intake level of severity and patient change scores at the session of interest (sessions 2 through 4 in Figure 4.3). The client is then located in the matrix that determines that he or she is a signal-alarm case (yellow or red area of the matrix), or satisfactorily progressing (green area of matrix), or ready for termination (white area of matrix).

The Empirically Derived Method

In an attempt to improve the rationally derived decision rules, Finch, Lambert, and Schaalje (2001) developed a parallel method for identifying cases for review based on statistically derived expected recovery curves that are more consistent with the methodology used in other quality management efforts, such as those developed by Leuger et al. (2001) and Kordy et al. (2001).

The empirical method used data drawn from numerous sites that were collapsed into a national database for research using the OQ-45. The database included 11,492 clients who in most cases completed the OQ-45 at each treatment session. Data from this sample were analyzed so that expected treatment recovery curves could be generated and thus could later be used as tools to evaluate new patients receiving treatment on a case-by-case basis. A brief description of the methodology used in this study can facilitate an understanding of the conception of the recovery curves for this particular instrument, the OQ-45. It should also be noted that this type of research is relatively new. As a result, very few instruments have sufficient data available for rapid application in clinical settings. For the OQ-45, however, these data are available now.

Methodology Used to Generate Recovery Curves

When the overall pattern of change evident in this large sample was examined, a gradually decelerating growth curve similar to those identified in previous studies on recovery curves (Howard et al., 1986) was evident. This relationship appears to be quite common in psychotherapy outcome studies, illuminating the fact that larger doses, or number of sessions, are required to produce a higher percentage of recovered clients. Thus, more treatment generally leads to greater improvement for clients.

Ideally it would be possible to generate an expected recovery curve for every possible intake score on the OQ-45 between 0 and 180. Although the data set used for this purpose was large, it was not of sufficient size to be able to establish an individual recovery curve for each intake score because the statistical techniques require a larger number of cases for reliable modeling. OQ-45 scores falling at the extremes of the continuum are quite rare; therefore, the full range of scores was divided into distinct groups by percentiles. This approach yielded 50 groups identified by intake score, with no fewer than 220 patients in each band, representing approximately 2% of the total sample.

The resulting groups of data were then analyzed to produce expected recovery curves and tolerance bands for each group. The methodological details of this analysis require sophisticated mixed-model analysis and are not further delineated here. This type of analysis allows for different lengths of treatment among clients, missing data, and hierarchical relationships between therapists, clients, and sessions. In addition, the statistical output provides sufficient information to allow for the calculation of expected outcome at each session along with expected tolerance bands around the expected point at each session.

The tolerance interval is a quality control protocol often used in engineering applications. Tolerance intervals determine the probability that a given OQ-45 score at a given session will fall within a specified interval (e.g., between 80 and 64). Thus, the tolerance intervals allowed for the identification of OQ-45 total score values that have an established probability of falling outside of the upper and lower limits of the tolerance interval. These limits could be used to identify failing and recovering clients.

Tolerance intervals were calculated for the expected mean OQ-45 total score at each session. A two-tailed, 80% tolerance interval was created around each of the estimates, providing a cutoff score at each session for identifying patients who might be included in the 10% of clients likely to fail in therapy or drop out early. Next, a two-tailed, 68% tolerance interval was calculated for each expected mean by session number, providing a cut-off score for individuals whose progress in therapy was either above or below the expected recovery rate by at least one standard deviation. With each mean estimate and the upper and lower bounds for two-tailed 80 and 68% tolerance intervals calculated, it was possible to plot lines across the mean estimates of OQ-45 total scores for each session, as well as for each upper and lower bound of the tolerance intervals. This produced a visual representation of the expected recovery curve by OQ-45 total scores across each session centered within the upper and lower cutoff bounds of each tail of the tolerance intervals.

The Empirically Derived Warning System

The coefficients and tolerance intervals previously described form the core of the empirically derived warning system by providing table values and charts of predicted therapeutic gains, against which any given patient can be compared. After an individual has completed a given OQ-45 administration, the total score can then be compared to the corresponding session value for others beginning therapy with a comparable pretest score.

If at any session following intake the OQ-45 total score for a patient is within the 68% tolerance interval shown on the chart, then therapy is proceeding as anticipated for this particular patient and a green-light message can be given as feedback. If the OQ-45 score falls outside of the upper 68% tolerance interval (upper 16%) but is still within the upper bound of the 80% tolerance interval, the patient is beginning to deviate by greater than one standard deviation from what is expected of a typical person at this point in therapy. As a result, the therapist would receive a yellow message as a warning to attend to this patient's progress. This one standard deviation unit approximates a 14-point increase in the OQ-45 score (a marker for reliable change). If this same OQ-45 score falls above the upper limits of the 80% tolerance interval (upper 10%), then the patient is deviating significantly in a negative direction from what is predicted for patients at this point in therapy, and his or her recovery curve is within the range of scores predicted for the 10% of patients whose progress is most in question. The 10% boundary is consistent with the estimate that about 10% of patients deteriorate following psychotherapy (Lambert & Bergin, 1994). At this point, the therapist would receive a red warning message that therapy may be heading toward an unsuccessful conclusion and that the therapist needs to consider an alternative course of action. As with the rationally derived method, those patients who receive either red or yellow warnings are referred to as signal-alarm cases.

A similar pattern can be described for scores falling below the lower side of the regression line. If the OQ-45 score falls below the lower bound of the 68% tolerance interval, then therapy is judged as proceeding better for this patient than is typically expected. At this point, the therapist would receive a white message that the patient is quickly progressing toward a termination point (a different message than that used with the rational method). If the same OQ-45 score falls below the lower bounds of the 80% tolerance interval, then this individual is deviating significantly in a positive direction from what is normally expected for a specific individual at this point in therapy, and the therapist would receive a blue message. At that point it is unclear what factors might be involved in this rapid alleviation of symptoms denoted by the blue signal. Possible explanations might include a so-called flight into health or other unrealistic reflections of resistance, medications beginning to work, significant reductions in psychosocial stressors, or simply a very rapid response to psychotherapeutic interventions.

As an illustration of how the empirically derived method can work in clinical settings, Figure 4.4 depicts a sample graph or quality management chart of a patient who scored an 87 on the OQ-45 at intake and whose response to treatment was plotted across 20 sessions. Therapy proceeds along the expected course for this moderately depressed patient, with worsening occurring at the sixth session. At this point in therapy, the patient had just lost her job, thus contributing to her deterioration in functioning. Over the ensuing weeks she had several job offers and was able to return to work. This patient then continued to make progress through ses-

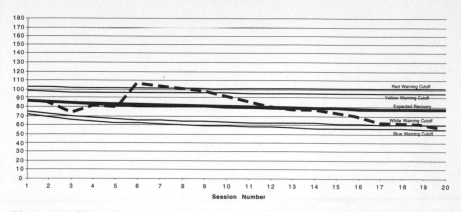

Figure 4.4 Client Progress in Comparison to Quality Management Cutoffs

Source: Reprinted from Finch, A. E., Lambert, M. J., & Schaalje, B. G. (2001). Psychotherapy quality control: The statistical generation of expected recovery curves for integration into an early warning system. Copyright 2001 by John Wiley & Sons. Reprinted with permission.

sion 16 as she had returned to the green zone. Using this system, the therapist would be given a white signal at session 17 indicating that it might be time to terminate treatment. The patient continued to improve through the 20th and final session.

This same type of monitoring (and extending into management) can be applied in practice. The clinician need have only one chart and two pieces of information: the initial score on the OQ and the current score on the OQ. Although the methods of analysis are rather sophisticated, the clinical application is quite simple.

The Rational and Empirical Method

To this point we have described two potential methods of identifying failing cases. Although not the main focus of this book, a brief excursion into a recent investigation that compared the rationally derived and empirically derived methods of identifying cases may be instructive. The comparison study illustrates that both methods accurately identify failing cases and compares their ability to identify failing cases quickly and accurately. Lambert, Whipple, Bishop, et al. (in press) compared the rationally derived and empirically derived methods of identifying cases for review. The major questions addressed were

1. How well do the respective methods predict treatment failure?
2. Do the methods agree on the cases that are given alarm signals?
3. Is there a tendency to over- or underidentify more or less disturbed patients as signal-alarm cases?
4. Is there a difference between systems in the speed with which they identify cases for review?

These latter two questions were seen as important because poorly responding cases tend to drop out of treatment early and must be identified as soon as possible if modifications to ongoing treatment are to be made. In addition, it is important to be especially careful to identify patients who are within the ranks of the most disturbed. These clients are sufficiently distressed that they have trouble finding relief. This difficulty, coupled with such clients' high level of initial disturbance, places them at special risk for problems such as suicide, difficulties with family, and work functioning difficulties.

In order to investigate the effectiveness of both approaches, data were analyzed for 492 clients who returned for more than one session and who took the OQ before each therapy session. So that feedback about their functioning could not bias results, the clients' data were stored electronically and were not shared with the therapist or client. For the purpose of this study, the dependent variable defining outcome was reliable worsening (deterioration), defined as a 14-point negative change. In the case of patients who started therapy in the functional range (i.e., below 64 on the OQ), in addition to getting worse by 14 points, they also had to leave therapy with a final score of 64 or higher, placing them in the dysfunctional range.

As can be seen in Table 4.3, of the 492 clients who entered treatment, 36 (7.3%) were reliably worse or had a deteriorated condition at termination of treatment. The rational method identified 81% of these cases ($N = 29$)

Table 4.3 Comparison of Predicted versus Actual Treatment Failure by Rationally and Empirically Derived Classification Methods

Actual Outcomes	Classification Method	Predicted Outcomes, N (%)		
		Positive	Negative	Total
		Hits	*False Negatives*	
Positive	rational	361 (79.2)	95 (20.8)	456 (92.7)
	empirical	373 (81.8)	83 (18.2)	456 (92.7)
		False Positives	*Hits*	
Negative	rational	7 (19.4)	29 (80.6)	36 (7.3)
	empirical	0 (0.0)	36 (100.0)	36 (7.3)
Total	rational	368 (74.8)	124 (25.2)	492 (100.0)
	empirical	373 (75.8)	119 (24.2)	492 (100.0)
Hit rates				
hits	rational			390 (79.3)
	empirical			409 (83.1)
misses	rational			102 (20.7)
	empirical			83 (16.9)

Source: Adapted from Lambert, M. J., Whipple, J. L., Bishop, M., Vermeersch, D. A., Gray, G. V., & Finch, A. E. (in press). Comparison of rationally and statistically derived recovery curves for improving the quality of patient care. Copyright 2002 by John Wiley & Sons Limited. Reprinted with permission.

whereas the empirical method identified all 36 (100%). The rational method correctly identified 79% of the so-called successful cases; the empirical method identified 82%. Overall the rational method correctly identified (hit rate) 79% of the clients, compared to 84% for the empirical method, a difference that was not considerably significant. These findings suggest that both methods could identify cases for review well above base-rate expectations, but that the empirical method was superior to the rational method in identifying treatment failures. Impressively, the empirical

> ### DON'T FORGET
>
> Patients who ultimately fail to benefit from psychotherapy can be identified early in treatment by both rationally and empirically derived methods.

method identified all 36 deteriorators, or people who got worse by the end of treatment, and the vast majority of the deteriorators (86%) were identified by the third treatment session.

Despite the accuracy of the rationally derived and empirical methods, both methods misidentified a significant portion of clients as signal-alarms who did not go on to deteriorate. However, the relatively high incidence of false alarms has a small cost in clinical situations. Unlike some medical decisions in which the cost of overidentification of signal cases may result in very intrusive interventions, the signal-alarm as it is typically used in psychotherapy merely alerts the therapist to the fact that the client is not progressing as expected; this suggests the need to reconsider the value of ongoing treatment but does not mandate specific changes to ongoing treatment. Thus, the signal-alarm is seen as supporting rather than supplanting clinical decision making. False alarms in other clinical decision making tasks can be much more problematic (e.g., they may signal expensive medical tests, surgery, etc.). Because the signal-alarm alerts therapists to the possible need for action as opposed to triggering a negative chain of events such as termination or referral, the current level of misidentification would seem to be tolerable. Thus, if a clinician is to err, false alarms are preferable to false identification of patients as getting better when in fact they are not. The latter would possibly lead to premature termination in situations in which the patient could benefit from continued treatment. Nevertheless, with either system therapists need information about the degree to which false alarms exist so that they can adjust their decision making accordingly.

Although the false-alarm individuals were identified as signal-alarm cases but never deteriorated, many of these individuals did not change following treatment. Indeed, a comparison of false alarms with individuals who were never signal-alarm cases indicated that the false-alarm cases had poorer outcome even though they did not ultimately deteriorate. As can be

Table 4.4 Outcome of Misclassified Signal-Alarm Cases

	Recovered & Improved	No Change	Reliably Worse[a]	Total
Rational Method (signal-alarm)	22 (23.2%)	73 (76.8%)	0 (0%)	95 (100%)
Rational Method (no signal-alarm)	180 (49.9%)	173 (47.9%)	8 (2.2%)	361 (100%)
Empirical Method (signal-alarm)	15 (18.1%)	61 (73.5%)	7 (8.4%)	83 (100%)
Empirical Method (no signal-alarm)	187 (50.1%)	185 (49.6%)	1 (0.3%)	373 (100%)

[a]These patients started treatment below 64 and got 14 points worse, but their final OQ scores were not 64 or more; they were therefore not considered deteriorated.

Source: Adapted from Lambert, M. J., Whipple, J. L., Bishop, M., Vermeersch, D. A., Gray, G. V., & Finch, A. E. (in press). Comparison of rationally and statistically derived recovery curves for improving the quality of patient care. Copyright 2002 by John Wiley & Sons Limited. Reprinted with permission.

seen in Table 4.4, the ultimate outcome of false alarm cases (from both the empirical and rational methods) was most often no change. While approximately 20% of the false alarm cases actually improved, very few of the false alarm cases reliably deteriorated (8% and 0% for the empirical and rational methods respectively. This suggests that the costs of a false alarm are minimal. These findings, taken together (signal alarms result in many treatment failures and false signal alarms have poorer outcome), offer further support for the signal-alarm methods.

In concert, the two methods identified 79 patients as signal-alarm cases (potential treatment failures). Examining signal-alarm cases in the 79 clients identified as signal-alarm cases by both methods provided a basis for discovering which method identified cases most rapidly. This issue is important because it deals with the speed with which therapists can be alerted about possible problems in the client's response to therapy. Of the 79 signal-alarm cases identified by both methods, 30 (38%) were first iden-

> **DON'T FORGET**
> ....
> Rational methods appear to be slightly quicker to identify failing cases than the empirical method.

tified by the rational method, one (1.3%) was identified by the empirical method, and 48 (60.8%) were simultaneously identified. These data suggest that when the rational algorithms are applied after the first treatment session, they are quicker to identify patients who are predicted to have a poor treatment response.

The Rational and Empirical Methods Reviewed

The Lambert, Whipple, Bishop, et al. (in press) study was based on the assumption that the development of clinical decision tools would assist the practicing clinician in identifying patients who are not responding to treatment and that such identification would lead to improved decision making and ultimately to better outcomes for these patients. It is an in-depth look at how outcome assessment can lead to sound clinical decisions. The evaluation and refinement of decision tools were seen as the primary goals of the research. Feedback to therapists based on a rational method of identifying specific cases at risk for treatment failure (developed through the consensual opinions of "expert judges") has been shown to be effective in improving patient outcome in two previous studies (Lambert et al., 2001; Lambert, Whipple, Bishop, Vermeerach, et al., in press). These studies are briefly described in Chapter 1. The development of a statistically based method for accomplishing the same goal (Finch, Lambert, & Schaajle, 2001) resulted in the need to compare the two methods and examine their relative value.

Results from these studies suggest that the identification of failing cases can occur quite accurately and rapidly and that the identification of failing cases, when fed back to therapists, results in improved outcomes and more efficient use of treatment. Although these studies do have limitations based on the samples, treatment settings, and methods, the information acquired to date has been found to be useful in clinical practice in that it provides data that can guide clinical practice with an adequate degree of accuracy. The clinical tools (both rational and empirical) used in the Lambert et al.

(2001) study are available at a nominal cost (contact apcs@erols. com or call toll free 1-888-537-2673). The graphs used to classify clients as white, green, yellow, or red based on the rational rules are reproduced here for the reader's convenience (instructions provided in Rapid Reference 4.4). Although research is needed to verify these findings before they can be advocated with confidence, the clinical application of the decision tools has very few drawbacks.

≡*Rapid Reference 4.4*

Figures for classification are used by entering the figure on the left side based on the client's intake OQ score. After the designated range of sessions completed by the client (e.g., 1 to 4), their change score from intake is calculated and the figure is entered at the point of difference (e.g., a patient who begins treatment with a score of 80 and gets +6 points worse will be given a green code).

With these figures in hand, the clinician can begin to identify which of his or her clients can be expected to have a positive outcome and which appear to be having a poor treatment response. If past research holds up, the use of this information will reduce failures from an expected ratio of 9 in 10 for the signal cases to one or two in four cases; that is to say, without feedback only 1 in every 10 red and yellow cases has a positive outcome, but with feedback one fourth to one half of these cases are predicted to have a clinically significant benefit.

SUMMARY

The potential methods of using outcome measures to aid with the initial assessments, tracking session-by-session improvement, and enhancing treatment for failing cases have been illustrated. As you may recall from the introduction of this book, the statistical modeling described in this chapter may be quite difficult to replicate for some, but the therapist need not completely understand the calculations as long as the principles of the techniques are understood. The reports generated from the models are easily used by clinicians and potentially helpful for clients.

The procedures described in this chapter were designed by clinicians for clinicians so that they can be easily applied to current practices. Clinicians can administer various measures at intake and over time not only to track client progress, but also to guide treatment and alert themselves to problems that may be arising. Aggregate data gathered in prior research studies such as those highlighted with the OQ-45 can serve as ammunition for the clinician so that decisions are made with the aid of strong research underpinnings. Armed with the knowledge provided by databases and norm groups, clinicians can obtain feedback regarding the client's current progress in relation to how treatment should be progressing, normatively speaking. Furthermore, in the most difficult of cases, with clients who do not improve at first, clinicians can see the degree to which treatment is deviating from the expected course, and changes can be made. If used appropriately, outcome assessment can not only inform clinical practice, but also can revolutionize the field of behavioral health treatment by helping keep clinicians, program directors, and insurance companies informed of the progress of current practice.

🐟 TEST YOURSELF 🐟

1. **Which phrase best applies to the utilization of outcome assessment data (client progress or lack of progress) to make changes in treatment?**

    (a) magnifying outcome

    (b) measuring outcome

    (c) monitoring outcome

    (d) managing outcome

    (e) none of the above

2. **What of the following information is provided by outcome assessment instruments?**

    (a) initial level of problem severity

    (b) client immediate needs

    (c) client target complaints

    (d) client strengths

    (e) all of the above

3. **What is an advantage of including target complaints in an outcome assessment?**

   (a) Target complaints provide a standardized measure of assessment.

   (b) Inclusion of target complaints serves to include the client in treatment and may build rapport.

   (c) Inclusion of target complaints ensures that clinicians provide appropriate interventions.

   (d) Endorsement of target complaints helps clinicians to utilize the client's personal strengths.

   (e) Target complaints can take the place of global measures of outcome.

4. **When therapists are interested in gauging meaningful change, they should assess the _____ of treatment effects on a client.**

   (a) least significant difference

   (b) most significant difference

   (c) statistical significance

   (d) clinical significance

   (e) none of the above

5. **What percentage of therapy clients leave treatment with a positive outcome?**

   (a) more than 90%

   (b) 80 to 90%

   (c) 40 to 70%

   (d) 20 to 30%

   (e) less than 20%

6. **What patient-oriented method incorporates the use of information about early response to treatment, dose response, and clinically significant change to identify signal-alarm or possible failing cases in therapy?**

   (a) rationally derived method

   (b) empirically derived method

   (c) statistically derived method

   (d) clinically derived method

   (e) medically derived method

(continued)

7. Which of the following best describes the empirically derived method?

(a) a patient-oriented approach that utilizes archival data about hospital stays, therapy appointments, and medication prescribed to generate patient profiles

(b) a patient-oriented approach that utilizes clinician judgment to construct at-risk patient profiles for treatment.

(c) a statistical method that has been shown to be superior to the rationally derived method in all areas.

(d) a statistical method that has been shown to be inferior to the rationally derived method in all areas

(e) none of the above

8. Patients who fail to benefit from psychotherapy can be identified by which of the following techniques?

(a) the rationally derived method

(b) the empirically derived method

(c) a structured clinical interview

(d) both a and b

(e) both a and c

9. Which of the following is an advantage of the early identification of failing cases in psychotherapy?

(a) more streamlined, efficient usage of therapy time

(b) more likelihood of success for those who are not failing cases

(c) failing cases can be terminated earlier on by therapists

(d) less outcome assessment will need to be done in future treatment

(e) none of the above

Answers: 1. d; 2. e; 3. b; 4. d; 5. c; 6. a; 7. e; 8. d; 9. a

Five

OTHER CLINICAL APPLICATIONS OF OUTCOME DATA

In addition to the important tasks of monitoring patient progress and identifying potential treatment failures, outcome monitoring can be used to create reports that go to outside contractors and payors such as managed-care organizations, administrators (e.g., evaluating therapist or program effectiveness within an agency), reporting public accountability in community mental health, or marketing mental health services. Like feedback on the progress of specific patients, many of these reports can improve the quality of clinical services through aggregation of individual change data. Several types of aggregation and reporting are described in this chapter along with other potential uses of outcome data that extend beyond the tracking of individual change.

AGGREGATION OF CHANGE DATA ACROSS THERAPISTS

Despite the current trend to assign specific techniques in the treatment of specific disorders, many reviews (Lambert & Ogles, in press; Luborsky, Singer, & Luborsky, 1975; Smith, Glass, & Miller, 1980; Wampold, 2001) have not found compelling evidence that patient change is dependent upon specific interventions or techniques. In fact, a consistent finding among these reviews is the relative equivalence of different types of therapy. Even though practitioners use a wide variety of techniques and espouse a broad range of theoretical orientations, there seems to be a generally positive effect from psychotherapy (Lambert & Ogles, in press). The impact of the individual therapist's contribution to psychotherapy outcome has only been examined in a few select studies. Nevertheless, strong evidence suggests that the individual therapist is a contributing factor in psychotherapy outcomes. Our review of the literature suggests the following:

- A wide degree of variability exists among the outcomes of therapists. Even when treatment manuals and other methods of controlling between-therapist variation are employed, a broad range of outcomes for different therapists is observed.
- Evidence supports the notion that some therapists are generally effective across patient types and severity levels, and that others are effective only with certain subpopulations.
- In many cases, the size of therapist effects is greater than what could be attributed to differences in treatment type alone.
- This area of research, although apparently ripe with possibility, has gone largely unexamined for the past decade. A number of reasons for this are possible, including the current trend toward empirically validated therapies and the use of treatment manuals.
- Most of the studies in this area examine a small number of therapists and patients. In fact, studies of the therapist's effects typically involve fewer than 30 therapists as participants with fewer than 10 patients each. This lack of sample size poses a problem as to the generalizibility and validity of findings in this area.
- Many of the findings in this area have been serendipitous. Evidence for the importance of the individual therapist is often found in work attempting to answer other research questions, such as the contribution of client variables to positive outcomes (Garfield, 1994; Beutler, Machado, & Neufeldt, 1994). In fact, the therapist's individual contribution to outcome is often only brought to light because of the failure to find powerful main effects of treatment types. The existence of exceptional therapists is not expected in a tightly controlled study and analysis of therapists is done almost as an afterthought. The possibility of examining therapist performance in the clinical setting, however, is one potential use of outcome data that may be especially appealing to

administrators and supervisors. Clinicians would naturally be reluctant to engage voluntarily in an evaluation of their performance that is based on client outcomes. The clinician could argue that such evaluations include a myriad of circumstantial and client factors which also affect outcome and may not represent therapist performance. At the same time, therapist performance as examined or averaged over a larger number of clients may help to alleviate some of these concerns. As we shall shortly see in at least one sample, most therapists have an average level of success; more rarely, therapists are exceptionally successful or very poor.

Orlinsky and Howard (1980) were the first to use outcome ratings of therapists to give therapists consumer ratings, so to speak (see Rapid Reference 5.1). The cases (143 women) seen by 23 therapists who offered a range of traditional verbal psychotherapy were carefully examined and therapists were rated. Of the 23 therapists in the study, 6 were rated *check +*, which was given when 70% or more of their cases were improved and fewer than 10% deteriorated, or when 40% of their patients improved "considerably" with no cases getting worse. Five received an *X* rating, which was given when 50% or fewer of their cases were rated as improved and more than 10% were rated as worse. These ratings, however, tell only part of the story.

In examining therapist factors that could be used to predict outcome, few relevant variables were discovered. Although professional degree and age were not related strongly to outcome, experience beyond 6 years was associated with better results. Retabulation of this data suggested the following

≡*Rapid Reference 5.1*

When routine outcome assessment procedures are in place, aggregating data for individual clinicians may provide information regarding their performance. Studies of therapist effects suggest that some clinicians have higher rates of client improvement. At the same time, all therapists had some clients who improved. This suggests that some therapists have limited range. Aggregated client outcome data within therapists may help inform therapist supervision, management, and employment.

estimates: 9% (2 of 23) of the therapists registered consistent low-level re-sults, while another 13% (3 of 23) showed mixed results. The improvement rate for the clients of these therapists was 44% (11 of 25 patients). In con-trast, just over 25% (6 of 23) of the therapists had excellent results, averag-ing just over 81% improving (35 of 43). Some therapists did well with the most difficult cases, whereas others did not. Notably, Orlinsky and Howard suggested that therapists who produced poor outcomes (on average) did not perform poorly across all cases. The data clearly demonstrated that these less effective therapists did well with some people. Thus, many of the therapists studied by Orlinsky and Howard (1980) were seen as being lim-ited in the *range* of patients with whom they were effective, rather than be-ing poor therapists in the absolute sense.

If nothing else, the Orlinsky and Howard (1980) study demonstrates the feasibility of examining the client outcomes of the individual therapists and providing consumer information that could be used in the referral process, for supervision, or in agency training. Naturally, the administrators of the agency may wish to provide ongoing training, remediation, or other con-tinuing education to assist the therapists with more limited ranges.

Summing data within practitioners is a natural extension of tracking pa-tient treatment response as presented in Chapter 4. Reports of such aggre-gated data for individual therapists have been recently published (e.g., Callaghan, 2001; Clement, 1996) and provide examples of the potential of such data. These efforts, when undertaken by an independent, private prac-titioner pose little threat. When the data are collected by others (e.g., su-pervisors, administrators, managed-care providers), however, the use of such information requires considerable trust in those who have access to the data. Examining and comparing outcomes across therapists is the most direct method of providing managed care and administrators with evi-dence of effectiveness and the likelihood that a referral to a particular ther-apist will result in a positive outcome for the patient. Therapists are likely to be mistrustful of such comparisons. As a result, clear guidelines for ac-cess to and use of the data must be determined in advance. If the data are used thoughtfully and carefully, therapist data may improve the quality of services without unnecessarily authoritarian uses of the data. This position stands in contrast to the illusion that the use of a so-called empirically supported psychotherapy guarantees a positive patient outcome. Although the use of empirically supported therapies is to be encouraged, it is not a substitute for monitoring patient progress.

> **CAUTION**
>
> Do *not* aggregate data within therapists without a clear understanding of how the data will be used, who will have access to it, and the like. Obtain written consent from providers. Otherwise you will run into serious resistance to and even noncompliance with future data collection tasks.

Three studies in which therapists used the Outcome Questionnaire-45 (OQ-45) to monitor patient progress have been reported in the literature, providing examples of useful methods. The first study reports outcomes in a private practice compared with a training-clinic benchmark. The second example reports outcomes in a private practice that includes child, adolescent, and adult patients, the outcome of which is benchmarked against national normative data. The third example includes an analysis of clients seen by more than 50 practitioners who all worked in the same clinic. The outcome of practitioners is compared with outcomes for the clinic as a whole with special reference to unusually effective and ineffective therapists. These examples demonstrate the types of reports that could be generated using aggregate data for the evaluation of therapists and contracting with managed care entities.

Outcome of a Training Clinic and a Therapist in Private Practice

This study (Lambert, Okiishi, Finch, & Johnson, 1997) compared the outcomes of a large student therapist population to the outcomes of a single private practitioner (Dr. L. Johnson). There were 36 student therapists who saw at least one client each week. Client progress was tracked using the OQ-45. The student data were used as a baseline comparison to the single private practitioner.

Outcome data were collected from 27 consecutive patients of the private practitioner over a period of a few months. Like the student sample, patients' diagnoses covered a broad range of disorders including dysthymia, anxiety disorders, adjustment disorders, major depression, and substance abuse. The 27 clients seen by the private practitioner began treatment with test scores typical of an outpatient sample, and those scores were similar to those of the student therapist sample.

Clients who saw this private practitioner (who used a solution-focused approach) recovered more rapidly than did the benchmark patients. For example, after two sessions, 36% of the private practice sample had met criteria for recovery (i.e., the Jacobson criteria for clinical significance described in Chapter 4), whereas only 2% of the student therapist sample had achieved similar results. After seven sessions, the private practitioner's patients had achieved results (43% recovered) that took almost three times as long (21 sessions) for patients seeing the student therapists to achieve.

Although the authors pointed out numerous limitations (e.g., no random assignment and a small number of clients seen by each of the therapists) the study still raises some interesting questions about the possible efficiency of the individual practitioner. The steep recovery curve produced by the private practitioner was much more rapid than that of the student therapists, even though they appeared to have equivalent client caseloads at intake (equivalent severity on the OQ-45). Again, this result highlights the possible existence of an exceptional (highly efficient) therapist. A graphic representation of outcome is presented in Figure 5.1. Data, such as these illustrated in the figure, were used by the brief therapist to assist in negotiations with managed-care organizations. As a result, he had a steady supply of client referrals, his practice was self-managed, and his paperwork was appreciably reduced.

To conduct a similar self-evaluation and produce a similar report, the clinician need only gather every-session data using a global client-report measure over a period of time. After a sufficient number of clients have participated in treatment (e.g., 25 or more), the therapist can begin to look at the number of clients that have reached the criteria for recovery. (Another possibility would be to use only one criterion for improvement—reliable change only—rather than using recovery criteria that include both reliable change and movement into the functional distribution.) For ex-

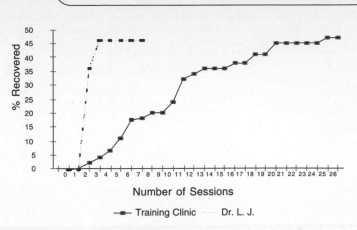

Figure 5.1   Therapist L. J. Compared to a University Clinic Sample

Source: Reprinted from Lambert, M. J., Okiishi, J. C., Finch, A. E., & Johnson, L. D. (1998). Outcome assessment: From conceptualization to implementation. Copyright 1998 by the American Psychological Association. Reprinted with permission.

ample, the clinician would calculate the percentage of the 25 clients that met recovery (or improvement) criteria after the second administration of the instrument (just prior to the second session), the third administration of the instrument, the fourth, fifth, sixth, and so on, until all sessions for the 25 clients have been covered. The percentages of recovered clients could then be graphed in a similar fashion to Figure 5.1 with percent recovered on the vertical axis and session number on the horizontal axis. The clinician could then use this graph when negotiating or establishing contracts or in other marketing functions. Similarly, the clinician may even use the graph in treatment to illustrate to the client the expected rate of improvement when participating in treatment. This may enhance client expectations of change and hopefulness about participating in treatment.

Of course a variety of potential hassles may limit the usefulness of such a graph. For example, clients with mixed diagnoses may not go together well in one graph. Clients with more chronic and persistent problems may unduly influence the expected outcomes. Indeed, the possibility of differences in caseloads among therapists is one of the major potential undermining variables that wreaks havoc on comparisons of therapists using client outcomes. If and when therapists are compared, it would be natural

≡ *Rapid Reference 5.2*

Case-mix adjustment involves the use of statistical methods for equating patient difficulty between comparison groups when random assignment of patients to groups has not been carried out. After data is case-mix adjusted, one can see what the outcome of different providers would be if they had equivalent caseloads.

for one therapist to say, "I have all eating disorder cases that are quite different from the mix of clients that are seen by other therapists." These concerns are reasonable and may indeed affect client recovery rates. At the same time, these differences can be taken into account statistically and rationally (e.g., case-mix adjustment; see Rapid Reference 5.2). The clinician can make separate graphs for long-term clients and brief therapy clients or use other strategies for displaying the outcomes. Likewise, rates of recovery for patients of a specific type (e.g., abused children) can be compared against rates of recovery for patients of the same type who see another therapist. The point remains that therapists may use aggregated data to illustrate client success rates when engaging in treatment with the clinician.

In a naturalistic setting, clients are not assigned to therapists at random nor through some prearranged systematic matching strategy, as they are in research. As in other analyses of therapy outcome in naturalistic settings, this difference poses a possible threat to the validity of the findings when attempts are made to make comparisons between clinicians with caseloads that are not formed via random assignment (Anderson & Lambert, 1995; Lambert & Okiishi, 1997). In order to counteract this problem, a *case-mix adjustment* strategy can be employed.

Case-mix adjustment is rooted in the idea that in the normal proceedings at a mental health setting, some clients will be more difficult to treat than others and therefore some therapists may carry a caseload that contains more difficult cases whereas other therapists will have easier caseloads. In order to balance for this unevenness in caseload, it is necessary to type or code client variables. This coding is the first step in making a case-mix adjustment.

Case-mix adjustment offers a substitute for random assignment and a way of compensating for the frequent occurrence in clinical settings of more difficult clients' being referred to therapists who have a reputation of enjoying such a challenge. It allows comparison of therapies within difficult and easy treatment cases by accounting for case difficulty (Brown, Dreis, & Nace, 1999; Marques, 1998).

Case-mix information can be used in two ways in this study. First, it can be used to balance caseloads so therapists seeing more difficult cases would have an adjustment in their expected outcomes. Second, it can be used to see whether therapists are differentially effective with certain types of clients. For example, although the outcomes for a therapist's overall case-load may appear to be average, when outcomes are broken down into meaningful groupings (e.g., severe, moderate, mild), it may come to light that a particular therapist is especially good at working with more, less, or moderately disturbed clients. This information could be particularly helpful for treating severely emotionally disturbed patients because some clinicians have a difficult time working with this population. If it is found that a clinician is particularly effective with clients who have severe emotional disturbances, then that clinician's services are even more valuable.

Within the current studies, the use of case-mix adjustment is not illustrated. Nevertheless, we have included a brief description in order to temper the potential comparison of therapists without considering the nature of their various caseloads.

Outcome of a Therapist in Private Practice

Asay, Lambert, Gregersen, and Goates (in press) reported on the outcome of patients seen in the private practice of a psychologist (Dr. T. Asay) whose clinical work consisted of treating both children and adults. In contrast to the effects of brief, solution-focused practice in the previous example, Dr. Asay practiced psychodynamic psychotherapy. He was trained as a clinical psychologist followed by 4 years of postgraduate training in psychodynamic psychotherapy. His treatment goals focused on helping clients gain insight and understanding into the origins and meaning of their problems by exploring past experiences, understanding unconscious processes, and analyzing resistance and transference reactions. Approximately half of his clients were children, and other approaches were incorporated (e.g., psychoeducation, cognitive, behavioral, and family systems) as deemed necessary with these clients.

Participants were 29 adults, 15 adolescents, and 25 children who consecutively entered treatment in his private practice during the period of the study. The majority of adult patients suffered from mood and anxiety disorders with 66% ($N = 19$) also receiving an Axis II personality disorder diagnosis. Eleven percent of the adults ($N = 3$) were diagnosed as psychotic. The child and adolescent clients received mood, anxiety, disruptive behavior, and adjustment disorder diagnoses. Adult clients completed the OQ-45 on a weekly basis after arriving 10 minutes prior to their scheduled session. The parents of the youth completed the Y-OQ on a weekly basis.

Scores from the weekly assessment were analyzed using survival analysis to predict the number of treatment sessions needed for each client group to meet the criteria for reliable change and clinically significant change according to the procedures recommended by Jacobson and Truax (1991).

The outcomes for adults and youth were compared and both groups' outcomes were compared with benchmark data from national surveys ($N = 1,395$) and research literature on clinical trials (Hansen, Lambert, & Forman, in press). Data analysis suggested that the youths were less disturbed (relative to normal controls) than the adult sample at the initiation of treatment.

Results indicated that for adults who started treatment in the dysfunctional range, 25% of the clients would be expected to achieve clinically meaningful change by the 42nd session of therapy, with 50% reaching criteria by the 54th session. Reliable change across the full adult sample was expected for 25% of the clients at the 11th session and for 50% after the 42nd session.

In contrast, 25% of youth clients were predicted to meet criteria for clinically meaningful change at the seventh session with 50% meeting criteria at the 14th session. Twenty-five percent of youth were expected to meet reliable change criteria at the 3rd session and 50% in seven sessions of treatment.

The percentage of adult clients who actually met criteria by the end of treatment showed that 18% improved, 25% recovered, 43% did not meet criteria for meaningful improvement or recovery, and 14% deteriorated. In the youth group, 30% improved, 43% recovered, 22% showed no reliable change and 5% deteriorated.

In comparison to national benchmarks, the degree of success (25% achieved recovery) with adult patients treated by Dr. Asay was superior to the national benchmark data, in which approximately 15% of clients (depending on the setting) met the criteria for recovery. No comparable benchmark data were available for the youth. In comparison to adult outcome, the youth clients achieved a much higher level of success. While the adults changed at a rate of 1.19 OQ points per session, the youth clients changed 3.43 Y-OQ points per session.

Two important differences between the benchmark data and Dr. Asay's data were noted. First, his adult clients were more disturbed than were the benchmark clients, as noted by the high percentage of clients with Axis II disorders. In addition, he kept his clients in treatment longer. His adult clients had an average of 23 sessions, whereas the benchmark clients received an average of 5 sessions.

After the data analysis, Dr. Asay decided there was value in monitoring client progress. He was pleased with the outcome of the youth he treated, but was determined to monitor and use early warning algorithms consistently with his adult cases.

Outcome of Therapists in a Counseling Center

Past research on therapists failed to categorize therapists on the basis of patient outcomes and relied solely on peer nomination procedures. In contrast, this study (Okiishi, Ogles, & Lambert, 2000) went in search of master therapists by reporting on the outcome of 56 therapists who worked in the same college counseling center. This study was aptly titled "In Search of Super Shrink," but essentially attempted to see whether therapists could be differentiated on the basis of their clients' speed and degree of recovery after adjusting for differences in caseload.

The client sample for this study consisted of college students seen at a large university counseling center for individual psychotherapy. Clients at the center presented with a wide range of problems from simple homesickness to personality disorders. The most common diagnoses in the final data set (see following explanation) were mood disorders ($N = 614, 34.5\%$), anxiety disorders ($N = 372, 20.9\%$) and adjustment disorders ($N = 305, 17.2\%$). Students were initially seen in a 30-min intake interview and then assigned to a therapist based on the client's needs and therapist availability. No experimental control was exercised over this routine procedure. Indeed, this data set is typical of what might be gathered in a counseling center or large group practice when gathering every-session client-report global outcome data. The range of sessions in this sample was 1 to 69, with a mean of 5.16 (SD = 7.2). Although 3,266 students were seen at the center over the 2-year period of data collection, the analysis being used for this study required at least three data points (a pretest and two additional measurements), so individuals with fewer than three treatment sessions including the intake were not included in the sample. This selection and exclusion criteria yielded a data set of 1,841 students. Ninety-one therapists contributed data to the entire data pool of 3,266 clients. Therapists who had data for fewer than 15 clients were excluded from the study. Using these criteria, 56 therapists were left who had seen a total of 1,779 clients. Data were also collected on a variety of therapist variables: level of training (preinternship, internship, and postinternship); type of training (clinical psychology, counseling psychology, social work); gender; and primary theoretical orientation (cognitive-behavioral, humanistic, psychodynamic). The modal therapist was a male, licensed, counseling psychology PhD who identified his primary theoretical orientation as cognitive-behavioral or behavioral.

The data from this sample were analyzed using a statistical technique called *multilevel modeling* or *hierarchical linear modeling* (HLM; Bryk & Raudenbush, 1992; Bryk, Raudenbush, & Congdon, 1996). To illustrate the process of HLM, a simple example is provided. Suppose therapist X saw 35 clients during the course of data collection. These clients were seen for varying numbers of sessions and had varying numbers of OQ-45 observations. Some clients provided data every week and others provided data more intermittently. Some clients attended a few sessions and others attended many. Although this type of complex data would be a major problem using other statistical techniques, HLM is ideal for a naturalistic study such as this, in that it accounts for missing and erratic data.

The first step of the HLM analysis of these 35 clients is to generate an *improvement curve* for each client. The curve is much like a regression line (or a single graph of client progress across sessions) and consists of a *y*-intercept, which in the case of this study, is an estimate of a client's initial or intake score on the outcome measure (OQ-45), and a standard error that is a measure of variability about the *y*-intercept. The curve also consists of a slope, which represents the rate of change across sessions, and a *t*-value, which is based on a comparison between the obtained slope and a hypothetical slope of zero.

The curves for clients seen by a single therapist have varying *y*-intercepts (intake scores), and slope estimates (rates of change) based on the scores for each particular client. The 35 recovery curves that are produced for these clients are combined statistically to produce one average recovery curve for therapist X. Again, this curve consists of a *y*-intercept (the average intake score of all 35 clients), and slope (the average rate of change for all 35 clients) estimate based on all of the individual clients' curves.

All of the therapist curves can be combined statistically to form one recovery curve for all the clients in the agency, seen by all the therapists, giving an indication of where clients, on average, started therapy and how their scores changed as a result of receiving treatment. Individual therapist recovery curves are then compared to see whether they differ significantly from the general recovery curve for all the therapists at the center. Individual therapist curves can also be compared to each other. In addition, separate curves can be created within the case-mix adjustment variable of client problem severity.

Returning to our study, we will recall that in this particular study, an initial analysis was performed taking into account therapist variables (i.e., level of training, primary theoretical orientation) before the main analyses were performed. This initial analysis was done in order to see whether some therapist variable other than the individual therapists themselves might be responsible for differences in clients' outcome. None of these therapist variables, however, accounted for the differences in initial scores or rates of improvement. These results are in line with studies suggesting that no one major theoretical orientation in therapy is more successful than another; they further suggest that any differences found between individual therapists are the result of other therapist variables.

Following this initial check of therapist variables, HLM was used to perform two analyses. In the first analysis, OQ-45 scores for clients were used to generate improvement curves within each therapist. After these combined recovery curves were computed, it was possible to see whether any significant variation appeared among therapists on their clients' initial OQ-45 scores to answer the question, *do some therapists see patients whose average initial disturbance is greater than other therapists?* Using these same curves, it was also possible to examine the rate at which clients' OQ-45 scores decreased in order to answer the question, *are there some therapists whose clients have better outcomes than others?*

When looking at the entire sample, clients' initial OQ-45 scores had an intercept of 73.79. That is, the average score for clients at intake was about 74—roughly 11 points above the clinical cutoff point for recovery, which was 63. The slopes, or rates of improvement for clients, had a mean slope of –0.79. The negative rate of change means the clients are improving (e.g., fewer symptoms each session with higher scores indicating more severe symptoms). This means that the average rate of change for a client per session was not quite one full OQ-45 point (about 0.79 of an OQ-45 point for each session in treatment). In short it would take roughly 14 sessions for the average client to move from the average intake score of 74 to the recovery point of 63. Figure 5.2 represents this growth curve graphically.

The analysis also indicated that significant variation occurred among the clients in both their average initial OQ-45 scores and in their rates of improvement; this suggests that clients showed a broad range of initial symptom severity levels and varying rates of improvement. A portion of these differences in intake scores and improvement rates may be attributable to therapists. As a result, further analysis examined differences among therapists.

When clients were grouped by therapist, there was no significant variation among therapists on their clients' average initial intake scores. This indicates that although clients differed significantly from one another initially

Whole Center

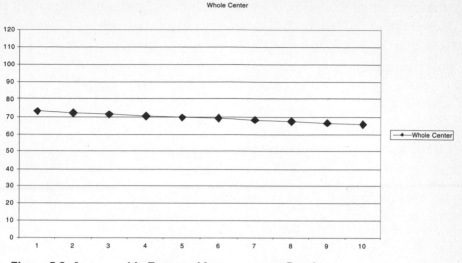

Figure 5.2 Agency-wide Expected Improvement Graph

Source: From Okiishi, Ogles, & Lambert (2000).

and represented a wide range of initial severity of symptoms, therapists had rather equivalent caseloads at intake. Since the intent of case-mixing is to balance for the effects of a nonrandom sample and unequivalent caseloads, this finding indicates that case-mixing, or adjusting for therapists' caseloads, was not necessary in this study.

However, the analysis indicated that therapists' clients differed significantly on their rate of change. The therapists' rates of improvement (i.e., the average rate of improvement for their clients) were quite different. For example, the therapist (A) whose clients demonstrated the steepest improvement slopes had an average drop of 7.97 OQ-45 points per session. This is 10 times the average rate of change for the entire center. The therapist (F) whose clients showed the least improvement actually had a positive slope, indicating that on average clients were endorsing more pathology at the end of treatment than when they entered treatment! This therapist's clients endorsed a higher degree of pathology, at a rate of 0.68 points a session. A graph of these two therapists' growth curves and the growth curve for the entire center is shown in Figure 5.3. As can be seen by examining this graph, the difference in outcomes between these two therapists is dramatic.

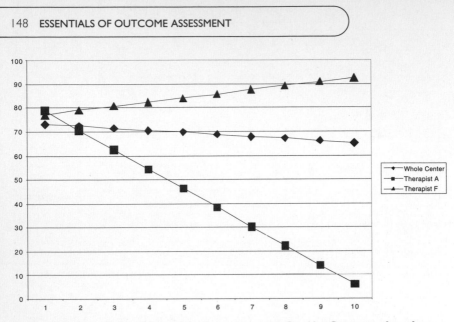

Figure 5.3 Two Therapists' Client Improvement Graphs Compared to the Agency Improvement

Source: From Okiishi, Ogles, & Lambert (2000).

Although these therapists had dramatic differences in the rates at which their clients changed, it is important to note the difference in the average number of sessions for each of the therapists. The average number of sessions for therapist A was .8 (SD = 1.88) and the maximum number of sessions was 10 (the session length of .8 is possible because intake sessions are considered session 0). This is much different from the average of 8.46 sessions (SD = 9.28) and maximum of 36 sessions of therapist F. Therapist A clearly saw clients for a much shorter time than did F.

The graph of therapist A and therapist F provides a dramatic example of differences between individual therapists. However, it is not necessary to go to these extremes in order to demonstrate the clear differences in therapist outcomes. Figure 5.4 is a graph of the top three therapists versus the bottom three therapists. Again, a stark contrast between the two groups is apparent.

Examining average session length helps further flesh out the picture of how these therapists practiced. The average number of sessions for the top three therapists was 2.4 (SD = 3.05), with a maximum of 16 sessions. The bottom three therapists had a mean number of sessions of 7.05 (SD = 8.75)

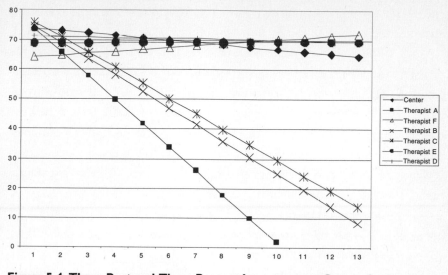

Figure 5.4 Three Best and Three Poorest Improvement Curves Compared to the Agency-wide Improvement Curve

Source: From Okiishi, Ogles, & Lambert (2000).

with a maximum of 54 sessions. As with the top and bottom individual therapists, the top three and bottom three therapists showed significantly different lengths of treatment. There were also significant differences in the number of sessions between the top third and the bottom two thirds of therapists. This finding suggests that the clients with the greatest rate of change were seen by therapists who saw them for shorter periods of time on average, a finding that parallels the study of trainees and the solution-focused therapist.

In order to synthesize findings for the entire sample and get a clearer picture of which therapists might be considered so-called supershrinks and pseudoshrinks, the average session length of individual therapists was multiplied by the slope of their recovery curve for each therapist. This provided an index of therapist exceptionality that takes into account both the rate of change and the average amount of time spent in therapy (high rates of change and higher numbers of sessions multiplied to make larger indexes).

Those therapists who might be considered the supershrinks and pseudoshrinks of this sample, using the criteria of total OQ-45 point change, suggested that therapist B saw clients an average of 3.77 times and the average gain for these clients was 20.77 OQ-45 points. Therapist G was a close second (although remarkably less efficient), seeing patients for 7.31 sessions while they improved an average of 19.37 points. Clients of therapists H and I also had remarkably good outcomes with average treatment gains of 18.02 points and 17.44 points (therapists G, H, & I are not shown in the graph). Interestingly, therapist A, who was considered to be the best therapist, so to speak, in terms of HLM slope, fell to 38th in the rankings when the data were examined in this way (due to a low average session rate).

On the bottom end of the spectrum, therapist F was still a clear standout as a so-called pseudoshrink. Therapist F saw patients for an average of 8.46 sessions (the 4th highest average) while these clients worsened by an average of 5.75 points. This is more than 5 points on average worse than the next to lowest–ranked therapist.

This analysis provided clear evidence that there are indeed significant differences among therapists regarding the outcomes of their psychotherapy clients. The analysis suggests that overall, clients seen at the center showed a broad range of initial severity of symptoms and varying rates of improvement. Clients had similar levels of symptom severity at intake within therapists. In fact, the similarity in degree of disturbance across therapist caseloads called into question the necessity of case-mix adjustments for the purpose of fairly contrasting therapists at this agency.

As expected (e.g., Beutler, Machado, & Neufeldt, 1994), there were no significant differences in client outcome among therapists based on the four therapist variables (gender, level of training, type of training, or theoretical orientation). This supports the idea that even though graduate school training and managed health care tend to focus on training in specific techniques, something else, perhaps the individual therapists themselves or their ability to connect with clients, is responsible for variation in client outcomes (Lambert & Okiishi, 1997).

Although therapists appeared to have roughly equivalent caseloads, there was a significant, sometimes staggering difference when improvement curves of clients within their caseloads were examined and compared to each other. There were also large differences between therapists when rate of improvement was examined in conjunction with average length of session. Both of these methods of defining outcomes provided very powerful evidence that, in fact, some therapists do have much better and worse outcomes than others.

A client seeing one of the top three therapists for their average session length of 2.47 sessions can expect to improve by about 15 points on the OQ-45. This is a reliable change (improvement) according to Jacobson's criteria. A client seeing one of the bottom three therapists for an average session length of 7.89 sessions could expect to get worse by about 5 OQ-45 points. The difference between these best and worst outcomes is 20 OQ-45 points, which is approximately 1 standard deviation in difference. Additionally, a person being seen by one of the best three could expect to complete therapy at a much more rapid rate. A client seen by one of the so-called best therapists could expect to be feeling significantly better after a few weeks of treatment. A client seen by one of the so-called worst therapists could expect to feel the same, if not worse, after almost three times as much treatment. This is powerful evidence that therapist differences do exist; the tricky part is deciding what to do with that evidence.

In this study, the results generated considerable discussion within the counseling center and created a possibility to offer therapists feedback on their overall effects in relation to other therapists. Because getting feedback was voluntary and the information was not given to administrators for their use, each individual therapist was free to seek feedback and remediation based on his or her judgment of the meaning of the research. Of course, much more ambitious use of the data could be initiated if therapists cared to trust the data for serious decision making. For example, because some therapists did show differential effectiveness with clients at different levels of disturbance, client assignment to therapists could be based on effectiveness rather than mere availability. Rank ordering therapists within client levels of disturbance and then using such ranking for treatment assignment decisions is, of course, unheard of, and possibly considered radical. Ironically, however, therapists frequently make referrals to other therapists in the absence of any information about the outcomes they obtain in their private practice.

Now, how does one make use of the findings of this study when assessing outcome in practice? The data presented in this example may be of little utility to the independent practitioner. A clinician who has the statistical sophistication could calculate his or her own average growth curve for his or her clients using the HLM procedures. This curve can be easily produced with a data set that includes the date, total score on the outcome measure, and client ID using the HLM program. If other client characteristics are included (e.g., diagnosis, age) in the data file, these variables can also be examined in relationship to client initial severity and rate of change. An independent clinician could gather the data, then calculate his or her average client rate of improvement. This information could then be used for marketing, contracting, or informing clients about expected improvement.

A more interesting use, however, may be the comparison of therapists within a group practice, agency, or managed-care panel. Although these comparisons should be tempered by differences in caseloads (e.g., through case-mix adjustment or other qualitative examination), data regarding the client outcomes may give one indication of therapist performance.

Therapists may resent being compared to other clinicians via client outcome data. To therapists, it may seem like an unnecessary invasion of privacy or worse—it may seem as though Big Brother is always assessing the quality of our services provided and the quality of our work is being questioned. Although these fears are understandable, at the same time therapists need to realize that in most cases they are already being compared with one another using other data gathered during treatment, such as number of recommended sessions, number of actual sessions, quality of treatment plans, client satisfaction ratings, rates of hospitalization for clients, and other utilization data. As a result, client outcomes may provide a more valid index of therapist performance than do pure utilization and process measures. In other words, if therapists are going to be compared, it seems that outcome data are the most valid and fair measure to use as a frame for comparison, provided that client caseloads are similar.

For the typical agency, the data analysis necessary for comparing therapists may be beyond current staff members' expertise. Some agencies are fortunate enough to have a staff member whose job description includes agency program evaluation. In many nonprofit companies providing mental health services, however, almost all resources must be used to provide reimbursable services. As a result, conducting this type of quality assurance analysis to compare clinicians to an agency average may be expensive, difficult, or both. We present it here because it is a potential use of the data that can identify clinicians who may need assistance, and information of this type may help to distribute cases to clinicians in a more meaningful way. Undoubtedly, some agencies will benefit from this example and its application.

USING OUTCOME DATA IN SUPERVISION

Outcome data may also be used in supervision. Clinicians who serve as clinical supervisors have the opportunity to enhance supervisory processes (and ultimately client outcomes) through the routine use of outcome data in supervision. Although much has been written about psychotherapy supervision (e.g., Bernard & Goodyear, 1992; Stoltenberg & Delworth, 1987; Watkins, 1997) and a considerable amount of research has been conducted about the effectiveness of supervision (e.g., Lambert & Ogles, 1997), little has been written regarding the potential use of outcome data to inform clinical supervision. Although many commonsense methods exist for using the outcome data to enhance supervision, little research has investigated the effects of supervision on client outcome and no research has been conducted on the impact of using client-rated outcome measures to inform clinical supervision. As a result, the suggestions considered here warrant further study.

Outcome data may be integrated into many of the routine tasks of clinical supervision. Three specific time points are especially relevant: the initiation of services, periodic review of ongoing cases, and end of services.

Initiation of Services

We have already illustrated how the initial data can be useful to the clinician. The collection of outcome data at intake can also be useful for the supervisor. Depending on the intake process at a given agency, initial outcome data may be useful to supervisors making decisions about case assignment, treatment planning, and allocation of services.

If initial outcome data is available to the supervisor prior to case assignment, the supervisor may review the data and reports generated, using the initial assessment data to identify client strengths, problems, and preferences. This descriptive information may be useful for making decisions about case assignment. For example, the supervisor may note that the client is a youth with externalizing behavior problems. As a result, a clinician who has a record of high-quality work with this type of adolescent may be assigned to the case. Similarly, clinicians who are in training or new to the agency may be assigned cases with fewer potential difficulties based on the initial assessment and the standardized outcome data.

In agencies that do not afford the supervisor an opportunity to be involved in treatment assignment decisions, the outcome data may still be useful to review with the clinician when reviewing the treatment plan in supervision. The initial ratings on the outcome instrument provide important assessment information. The supervisor may review the reports and forms with the clinician to help the supervisor judge the appropriateness of the therapist's treatment plan. These tools will be especially useful for the supervision of students in training. Generally, the supervision may take the form of examining the outcome ratings or reports with the clinician, identifying potential issues (strengths and target problems), planning with the clinician an approach for reviewing the issues with the client (including soliciting the client's feedback and preferences), and projecting the potential treatment issues and services that may be provided. The outcome forms give the supervisor firsthand information regarding the client's view of his or her most pressing problems and concurrent strengths. In agencies in which clinician verbal report is the primary format of supervision, the outcome data supply additional information regarding the client's perspective. These sources of information are combined to develop the treatment plan.

The outcome data can also be used to project the need for various services across the treatment spectrum and the potential intensity of such services. Individuals may report needs, problems, or strengths in a variety of domains that indicate potential provision of vocational, recreational, therapeutic, medical, or other services. Clinical supervisors can review the intake outcome ratings to help supplement other assessment data and supervisor reports when determining the types and intensity of services that the clinician will offer to the client.

In short, the outcome data provide a standardized rating of various domains that can supplement other clinical sources of data. These data can be used by the supervisor to match service providers with clients, judge the appropriateness of clinician-created treatment plans, and project the need for various types and intensities of service.

Periodic Review

Tracking client progress on goals and treatment issues using outcome instruments is the primary function of ongoing outcome assessment. Not only are these data useful to the client and clinician, but the clinical supervisor may also use the data to inform the supervisory process. A review of outcome tracking data may reveal cases in which clients are making progress, remaining stable, or deteriorating. This information allows the supervisor to make decisions regarding the selection of cases for review during supervision. High-priority cases can be identified for review based on both supervisor verbal report, outcome tracking data, or other information; this may help the supervisor to make more efficient use of supervision time—supervision can focus more on clients who are not making progress as expected.

After ongoing data entry procedures are in place, the clinical supervisor can review the progress of each client to identify progressing, deteriorating, or plateauing cases. Clearly, cases in which the client is reporting more symptoms, poorer quality of life, or dissatisfaction with services may require immediate focus with a greater portion of supervision time directed to making plans regarding appropriate interventions. Thus the focus of supervision could hinge on the findings from periodic reviews of client outcome.

Ending Services

When clients report improved functioning, fewer symptoms (or the capacity to cope with current symptoms), better quality of life, and so on, clinical supervisors may be alerted to the possibility that services might be gradually diminished or ended. Of course some clients will require medications or clinical support for extended periods of time. Nevertheless, the outcome data provide objective evidence of prolonged progress and may help the supervisor and clinician in making decisions regarding decreasing the intensity of services or terminating services. Once again, the outcome data give additional information to the supervisor so that he or she can better judge the appropriateness of the clinician's decision to end treatment with a given case. Lambert and Hawkins (2001) have elaborated on the use of outcome data in supervision and presented further examples of specific uses of such data.

A variety of other potential uses of outcome data both for the individual case and in aggregate form may be useful to the supervisor. We have addressed three potential uses of the data when initiating services, selecting cases for periodic review, and making decisions regarding the end of services. Intuitively, it seems obvious that outcome data could be helpful in the supervisory process. However, much research needs to address these uses of data in supervision because there is little current evidence that client outcome data are informative to the supervisory process. At the same time, both individual and aggregate data may be useful to the supervisor when making decisions regarding the current performance of the clinician.

OTHER USES OF AGGREGATE DATA

In addition to the evaluation of therapists and supervisor uses of data, a variety of other potential uses of aggregate data are available in practice. Perhaps the most noteworthy is the aggregation of data for a program or agency. When all session data are collected for all therapists within an agency, data can be aggregated to provide an overall picture of the treatment provided by the organization. For example, the percentage of clients who make clinically meaningful change could be calculated. The average rate of change per session could be determined. In addition, differences in clients referred from different sources (e.g., court, schools, medical settings) could be identified in terms of initial severity, length of treatment, and ultimate outcome. This type of analysis could be especially useful to an organization that has a contract with a specific business or entity. Data analyzed regarding the program's performance related to that contract could be used when renegotiating contracts or accounting for dollars spent. Finally, aggregate data analysis may also be prepared for publication and contribution to the scientific literature.

Routine outcome measurement can also be used to compare outcomes across practice groups, clinics, and those who contract with managed-care organizations. The value of such activities is that they allow such groups to examine and report the consequences of their treatment efforts; the activities also establish a baseline or benchmark of effects, which they can use to compare the impact of quality improvement efforts. Often efforts to improve the quality of services offered by provider groups is the domain of so-called clinical information systems developed by large managed-care corporations. Implementation of these systems has lagged far behind managed care's development of cost containment efforts. Nevertheless, a few managed-care companies have funded large-scale efforts to build outcome management systems (e.g., Bartlett & Cohen, 1993). Such efforts are also underway outside of managed care. For example, Barkham et al. (2001) are exploring such efforts within the National Health System of the United Kingdom. Kordy et al. (2001) have initiated similar outcome and quality management systems across Germany and within the European Economic Community. Although not yet well advanced, data are emerging that suggest that such efforts can be used to improve quality on a larger scale than efforts focused on the individual provider.

Two examples of outcome-driven quality management can help to illustrate the possibility of such systems.

The PacifiCare Behavioral Health Initiative (PBH)

PBH is a managed behavioral health company with a coverage of more than 3 million lives in both commercial and public-sector clinics in nine western states. Implementation of an outcome management system took place with a subsector of clinics in 1999. The company decided upon self-report as the basis for its outcome management system. This decision was based on cost considerations—primarily that clinician-based rating scales are time consuming and require training and retraining of clinical staff in order to acquire reliable data. In addition, clinicians tend to underestimate deterioration.

In keeping with the principle of minimizing the cost and effort of data collection, Lambert, Burlingame, and colleagues developed two 30-item self-report questionnaires—the Life Status Questionnaire (LSQ) and the Youth Life Status Questionnaire (YLSQ)—for the PBH outcome management program. Both the LSQ and the YLSQ have a range of possible scores from 0 to 120. Items were selected for the LSQ and the YLSQ on the basis of their tendency to improve during treatment while remaining relatively stable in a sample of matched control participants who were not in treatment. This approach resulted in instruments that were not only reliable and valid, but also sensitive to change over short time periods.

The LSQ and the YLSQ were used in PBH's outcome management program with 19 private-sector group practices and five public-sector clinics that provided outcome data. PBH's highest-volume solo providers also participated. PBH names its outcome management program the Algorithms for Effective Reporting and Treatment (ALERT) system. The ALERT system links the patient, the provider, and the PBH in an information loop that provides timely reports on critical risk factors and changing levels of patient distress. Aggregate-level reports summarize clinical outcomes for entire systems of care and for specific provider groups.

The ALERT system is based on an approach to data capture and management that retains maximum flexibility and timely reporting while minimizing cost. First, data are captured on paper forms that are faxed to a central location by means of the Teleform, a product of Cardiff Software, Inc., of Vista, California, that permits the user to design forms and then perform optical character and make recognition from fax- or scanner-produced images of the completed forms.

The performance indicators and decision-support tools are the most critical elements of an outcome management program. As noted, the key performance indicator is the change in the score on the LSQ or the YLSQ from one session to the next. However, this change is not highly informative unless we know what level of improvement it is reasonable to expect.

Outcomes are impossible to interpret without a valid method for statistically accounting for variations in the severity and difficulty of a case—that is, case-mix adjustment. A case-mix model uses data collected at intake to predict the change score at the end of treatment. Because severity of initial disturbance is an important factor in determining the rate of change and expected recovery, it is useful to divide the scores for patients into four severity ranges: normal (0 to 38), mild (39 to 51), moderate (52 to 64), and severe (65 to 120). The mean ±SD intake LSQ score for the PBH data repository was 53 ± 18, and the mean ±SD YLSQ was 41 ± 19.

Arguably, one of the most powerful methods for managing outcomes is a case-mix model that includes predictions of the trajectory of change (Lyons et al., 1997). Such a method depends on repeated measurements at regular intervals throughout treatment so that the progress of each patient can be monitored against these predictions. Obviously the development of valid case-mix adjustment and trajectory-of-change models requires a large normative sample of patients within levels of disturbance for which there have been repeated measurements.

The PBH outcome management program uses a repeated-measures design with the frequency of data collection greatest during the initial phase of treatment. Data are collected at the first, third, and fifth sessions and then less frequently, depending on the risk and complexity of the case. This repeated-measures design enables the trajectory of improvement to be tracked as part of the clinical management of the case. The trajectory during the first few sessions tends to be highly predictive of outcome (Brown & Lambert, 1998).

The PBH data repository provided the means to model the expected trajectory of change for the most common diagnoses in outpatient samples. A sample of more than 3,200 adults and 800 children and adolescents was used to calculate the expected change. The cases selected were drawn from more than 15,000 cases in the data repository and reflected the commercially insured population. The cases were selected on the basis of completeness of data, including the primary diagnosis, the score on the LSQ or the YLSQ at intake, and test score from at least one other assessment point.

The data repository also contains test protocols from community volunteers who are not currently receiving any mental health treatment. This sample was used to estimate a cutoff score between normal and clinically significant levels of life distress (Jacobson & Truax, 1991). The mean ±SD intake score for the clinical sample drawn for the PBH project was 82 ± 24. According to the formula, the cutoff score between the clinical sample and the community sample was 61. The system can thus track the improvement of each patient against that of similar persons in the normative sample. The cutoff score provides the means for determining the point at which a patient is within the normal level of life distress. This feature is critical to the success of the outcome management program and is one criterion for determining when patients are in need of continued care.

Their analyses of multiple outpatient samples indicated that the single best predictor of the change score for any given treatment episode was the score at the beginning of treatment. Other variables, such as diagnosis, chronicity, and treatment population altered the relationship to some degree, yet every sample analyzed during the course of the project produced the same result regardless of differences on these variables. The change score had an essentially linear relationship with the intake score—higher levels of distress at intake predicted higher change scores, but more shallow trajectories of recovery over time.

The ALERT system used a change index, which employed a residualized change score, calculated by subtracting predicted change from actual change for each case. Positive values indicated above-average results. Although the system tracks outcome for individual cases, it also provides regular reports of aggregated results across multiple patients for use by clinicians, clinical managers, and administrators. Two sets of outcome reports are provided—one for closed cases (Aggregate Outcomes report) the other for active cases (Change Index report). They are typically produced on a monthly basis, thereby providing both monitoring and managing capabilities. The Aggregate Outcomes report uses a change index based on the average of residualized change scores. It provides results for children and adults separately but in the same metric units (effect sizes) so as to help make the data comparable between the two groups. It also presents outcome by level of initial distress—as categorized into the quartiles previously discussed. The report provides information on number of patients treated, those with more than one session, average number of sessions per case, expected change based on the case-mix model, and actual change.

Table 5.1 presents data from the LSOQ and LSQ for a group of practitioners. The outcome as shown in this report suggests that the outcome for closed cases ($N = 288$) was above average in relation to the case-mix benchmarks. It was highest for moderately distressed child and adolescent patients (effect size (ES) = .22). The overall positive ES of .10 for all cases was significantly different from an ES of 0 at the 90% confidence level. Their clients' outcome suggest that their practice is performing better than expected, given its composition.

Human Affairs International (HAI)

This example also demonstrates the use of aggregate data by a managed health care company, Human Affairs International or HAI, that insured more than 10 million lives nationwide. Presented here are data collected from seven large provider groups (or clinics) who had contracts with the company to provide behavioral health services.

It was clear to HAI that patients differed in their pattern of improvement over time and in the number of treatment sessions necessary to return them to a normal state of functioning. Research had suggested that patient variables moderate outcome (Garfield, 1994), and that among variables that seemed most promising were severity of disturbance, history or prior diagnosis, complexity of symptomatic dysfunction (comorbidity), and motivation. The statistical models used could accommodate complex solutions for predicting final outcome. However, much of the variance was taken up by degree of initial disturbance, and this simple variable became central in case-mix adjustments. Like PBS, HAI used the effect-size statistic to express outcomes. The effect size can be interpreted as degree of change from intake to treatment termination in standard deviation units. Figure 5.5 illustrates the relationship between initial OQ-45 score and final outcome. As can be seen, those patients who began treatment with the lowest level of distress (bottom quartile) actually show a slight negative change

Table 5.1 Data from a Managed Behavioral Health Care Company's Aggregate Outcome Report

Age Group and Severity of Illness Expected	More Than One Data-Collection Point		Change in Score (effect size)		Change (Actual-expected)
	Number of Cases	Sessions per Case	Actual	Expected	
Adults					
Normal range ($N = 55$)	18	4.00	0.02	−0.03	0.05
Mildly distressed ($N = 60$)	45	5.50	0.21	0.20	0.01
Moderately distressed ($N = 49$)	28	6.55	0.65	0.49	0.17
Severely distressed ($N = 61$)	40	7.10	0.90	0.75	0.16
All ($N = 225$)	131	6.01	0.49	0.40	0.09
Children and adolescents					
Normal range ($N = 15$)	6	3.40	−0.06	−0.05	−0.01
Mildly depressed ($N = 13$)	6	5.00	0.40	0.23	0.17
Moderately distressed ($N = 18$)	9	7.20	0.55	0.33	0.22
Severely distressed ($N = 17$)	10	7.30	0.80	0.66	0.14
All ($N = 63$)	31	6.07	0.48	0.34	0.14
All patients ($N = 288$)[a]	162	6.02	0.49	0.39	0.10

Note: Patients included in the report began treatment between three months and 15 months before the date of the report (September 20, 1999). A 90% confidence level was used.

[a]The change index for the entire sample is above average on the basis of a significance level of $< .1$.

Source: From Brown & Lambert (1998).

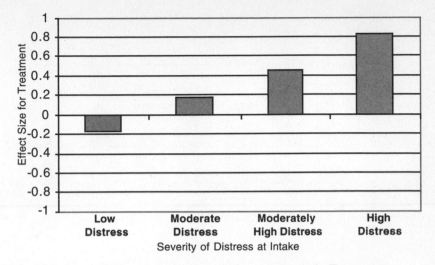

Figure 5.5 Level of Distress at Intake and Improvement in Treatment

as a group. In contrast, those who are most distressed at the beginning of treatment show the largest treatment gains. These data can be used to adjust expectation (case-mix adjust) for outcome for specific providers or for provider groups. For example, a provider whose treatment caseload is dominated by more high-functioning patients would not expect to see as much change (in patients) as a provider whose caseload is made up of more highly disturbed patients. Thus, if the outcome of patients seen by these two therapists were compared, some adjustment for their differing caseload would need to be taken into account (Brown & Lambert, 1998).

Figure 5.6 illustrates the use of this methodology by comparing the outcome of patients seen in seven different clinics (practice groups). The practice groups represented outpatient clinics across the United States. The expected level of what were called treatment gains for patients in each practice group, A to G, was based on their initial OQ scores. Based on these intake scores, practice group F's patients were expected to show the greatest gains, whereas practice groups C and G's patients were expected to show the least improvement.

Actual outcome was calculated by averaging the pretreatment to posttreat-

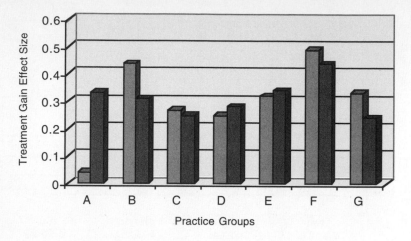

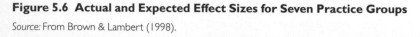

Figure 5.6 Actual and Expected Effect Sizes for Seven Practice Groups
Source: From Brown & Lambert (1998).

ment change scores for patients seen by providers in each practice group. In this evaluation of treatment outcome (Figure 5.6) we were able to compare each group's performance against expectancies for that group; we were also able to compare groups with each other to determine those that appear to be underperforming and overperforming. For example, it is clear that practice group A's patients achieve outcomes well below what was expected and also well below those of the other groups that had a similar mixture or patients.

These data could be used in very practical ways. For example, on the basis of this information and with the freedom to make a referral of a patient for treatment by clinicians working in practice group A or B, which would you choose? What could be learned about the treatment given by group B that could be shared with group A in order to make it more likely that patients treated by group A would have more positive outcomes?

Figure 5.7 breaks down the same information by taking into account the number of treatment sessions offered to each patient. In this figure, it appears that the relatively poor outcome of patients seen in group A is not a result of their having received too little treatment. These patients change the least on a session-by-session basis. After this information is fed back to

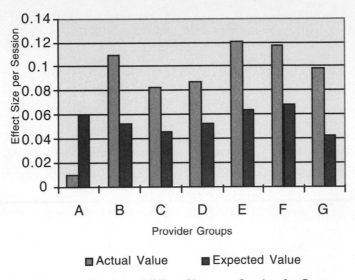

Figure 5.7 Actual and Expected Effect Sizes per Session for Seven Practice Groups

Source: From Brown & Lambert (1998).

group A, the process of quality improvement can be facilitated. The providers know there is a problem with patient treatment success and they can begin to take corrective actions.

It is early to see the value of having benchmarks for improving quality of outcomes. In this case a large data repository allowed for the development of expected treatment response and case-mix adjustment based on severity of patient disturbance. Expected treatment response represents an external standard with expectancies based on a large data set of over 5,000 patients. In addition each clinic can, over time, monitor the degree to which its actual outcomes show improvement—that is to say, trend towards better outcome.

SUMMARY

A variety of analytic methods and opportunities are available to the clinician when data are gathered for every client seeking treatment. Data for therapists, programs, and clinics can be tabulated, illustrated, and analyzed. Similarly, data regarding clients such as diagnosis, referral source, and other attributes can be used to provide information. These methods may be used for internal purposes to improve the quality of services or for external purposes to market or negotiate contracts for services.

Although multiple uses of aggregate data are available, they all require a greater amount of statistical expertise and time than is often available to the practitioner. As a result, we expect that the methods of data analysis explained in Chapter 4 may be more frequently used by clinicians in practice. Indeed, our repeated focus within this book has been on the use of outcome data for monitoring the progress of the individual client anyway. Nevertheless, it is important to include the potential uses of aggregate data for completeness of presentation. In the next chapter, we give some examples of both individual and aggregate uses of data for further illustration of the practical uses of outcome data.

➣ TEST YOURSELF ➣

1. **Which of the following most accurately reflects the findings of research on the individual therapist's contribution to psychotherapy outcome?**

   (a) Individual therapist differences have no bearing on outcome.

   (b) Individual therapist differences account for almost all of the differences in outcome.

   (c) Individual therapist differences account for some of the differences in outcome.

   (d) Therapist theoretical orientation is a more important factor than are individual differences.

   (e) None of the above.

2. **The Orlinsky and Howard study (1980) was important because the researchers found that less effective therapists, by way of comparison to more effective therapists**

   (a) have a limited range of patients that they can effectively treat.

   (b) have secondary skills that can be used with the child population.

   (c) have poorer outcomes no matter what type of patient they choose to treat.

   (d) should quit their day jobs.

   (e) should enroll in workshops designed to teach the skills used by more effective therapists.

3. **Why should clear guidelines for access to and use of within-therapist data be determined in advance of outcome assessment?**

(a) Patients will benefit more from knowing how the data will be used.

(b) Patients will be more open and responsive during the evaluation.

(c) Therapists will be less likely to utilize ineffective treatment methods and more likely to focus on hard-line evidence.

(d) Therapists will be less mistrustful of those collecting data and more likely to see the benefits.

(e) Therapists and patients will collaborate on a more effective treatment plan.

4. **Which of the following is true in regard to the appropriate usage of within-therapist recovery rates in therapy?**

(a) The clinician could use the recovery rate information when negotiating contracts for marketing purposes.

(b) The clinician could use the information in treatment with the client to convey the expected rate of improvement in treatment.

(c) Recovery rates could enhance client expectations of change.

(d) Recovery rate could influence client hopefulness.

(e) All of the above.

5. **Hal, a clinician who likes to see patients who present challenges to the therapist, is dissatisfied so far with the outcome assessments that have compared him to other therapists at his clinic. He has often said that the assessments do not take into consideration the differences in his caseload. He would be best served to use which design of the following in outcome assessments at his clinic?**

(a) random assignment

(b) pre-post design

(c) case-mix adjustment

(d) Bonferroni adjustment

(e) all of the above

(continued)

6. **The study that tried to determine who were the so-called supershrinks and pseudoshrinks found that**

   (a) Clients with the greatest rate of change were seen by therapists who were verbally gifted.

   (b) Clients with the greatest rate of change were seen by therapists who saw them for shorter periods of time on average.

   (c) Clients with the greatest rate of change were more compliant than were other clients.

   (d) Clients with the greatest rate of change were by and large more intelligent.

   (e) None of the above.

7. **The "supershrink versus pseudoshrink" study also found which of the following therapist variables to be key determinants of client outcome?**

   (a) therapist gender

   (b) therapist level of training

   (c) therapist theoretical orientation (with cognitive-behavioral being better)

   (d) prestige of the university where the therapist earned degree

   (e) none of the above

8. **Which of the following is the most productive way that outcome data can be used in supervision?**

   (a) Supervisors can use the data to indicate which clinicians should be promoted.

   (b) Outcome data can be used to save time so that weekly supervision meetings with clinical supervisors are no longer necessary.

   (c) Outcome measures can be filled out by the supervisor during the supervision process.

   (d) Outcome measures can supplement material discussed during routine supervisory meetings.

   (e) All of the above.

9. What has research on outcome data in supervision generally found?

(a) A paucity of research exists, but outcome data has the potential to enhance supervision.

(b) Supervision is useless without standardized outcome data.

(c) Outcome data should not be incorporated into supervision.

(d) A large of amount of evidence supports the usage of outcome data in supervision.

(e) Supervision should only be provided for difficult cases.

Answers: 1. c; 2. a; 3. d; 4. e; 5. c; 6. b; 7. e; 8. d; 9. a

Six

ILLUSTRATIVE CLINICAL EXAMPLES

A variety of potential uses of outcome data have been described in the previous two chapters. Chapter 4 focused more on the use of data for the individual client, whereas Chapter 5 examined potential uses of aggregate data. In this chapter several examples of both uses are provided.

EXAMPLE 1: INDIVIDUAL ADULT CLIENT

Dr. May Zurment (henceforth Dr. Z) decided to use the Brief Symptom Inventory (BSI) for the assessment of outcome with all clients receiving outpatient psychotherapy in her private practice. Dr. Z picked this inventory because it has several scales that assess various areas of symptoms along with the global scale that could be used for tracking change. Dr. Z has a part-time private practice that she operates out of shared office space within a group practice. However, she has no support staff. She does all her own clinical and billing paperwork.

Dr. Z decided to ask each client to complete the BSI as part of the initial paperwork that she asks all clients to complete prior to their first interview. In addition, she asks every client to come to each session a few minutes early to complete the BSI. She attached a small folder to the front of her office door to hold copies of the BSI. When clients come into the small foyer outside the office, they can take one of the forms and complete it even when she is still finishing up with another client.

Although Dr. Z gathers the data from every client at every session, she does not enter the data into a database. She scores the BSI immediately at the beginning of the session and graphs the total score on a tracking sheet for each client. Each client's chart includes a tracking form with the charted global scores over the course of treatment. When she has gathered data on 50 to 60 consecutive clients, she intends to enter the data in a database and look for patterns among clients or prepare a report concerning her overall effectiveness. For now, however, she is only using the data to assist with the treatment planning and monitoring of treatment for each client. The data for one of her clients, Jane Smith, are presented here to illustrate the way in which Dr. Z uses the data.

Ms. Smith completed the BSI prior to her first session while completing the initial paperwork. Dr. Z asked Ms. Smith to complete the BSI immediately after she completed the consent-for-treatment forms. Dr. Z then scored the Global Severity Index by hand while Ms. Smith completed some of the contact information and billing forms. Dr. Z waited to score the other scales until after the session. Ms. Smith's initial score on the Global Severity Scale was a raw score of 1.40 (the average rating on all 53 items or 74/53). The T-score for a raw score of 1.40 is 50 when compared to a sample of women in outpatient treatment and 70 when compared to non-patient women. Dr. Z noted that Ms. Smith's score was typical of outpatients seeking treatment and clearly within the clinical range.

Dr. Z had a set routine for looking at the individual items. In addition to scoring the Global Severity Index, she examined the items that covered the following content areas—thoughts of ending life, temper outbursts, feelings of being watched or talked about, feelings of hopelessness about the future, thoughts of death of dying, urges to beat or harm someone, and doubts of one's sanity. In addition, she asked specific questions about drug and alcohol use because items covering these issues were not included in the BSI. Ms. Smith's responses on these items are displayed in Table 6.1. Dr. Z noted that Ms. Smith had some thoughts of ending her life and thoughts of death and dying that were accompanied by feelings of hopelessness.

In addition, Dr. Z scanned the items looking for any that were endorsed as a 3 (quite a bit) or 4 (extremely). A cluster of seven items were endorsed

Table 6.1 Ms. Smith's Responses on Several BSI Critical Items

Item	Response
Thoughts of ending life	3 (quite a bit)
Temper outbursts	0 (not at all)
Feeling watched or talked about	0 (not at all)
Feeling hopeless about the future	4 (extremely)
Thoughts of death or dying	3 (quite a bit)
Urges to beat or harm someone	0 (not at all)
Something wrong with my mind	1 (a little bit)

as 3s or 4s. These items are displayed in Table 6.2. In addition, several items on the anxiety scale were also endorsed as 2s and 3s. Dr. Z noted that the most prominent theme in Ms. Smith's responses was one of depressive symptoms accompanied by some anxiety—perhaps a typical outpatient depression type of case.

During the initial interview, Dr. Z briefly discussed the assessment results, including the level of severity, some discussion and assessment of Ms. Smith's thoughts of self-harm, and selection of targets for treatment. The

Table 6.2 Ms. Smith's Responses on Several Items That Might Be Potential Targets for Treatment

Item	Response
Thoughts of ending life	3 (quite a bit)
Feeling hopeless about the future	4 (extremely)
Thoughts of death or dying	3 (quite a bit)
Feeling blue	4 (extremely)
Feeling no interest in things	4 (extremely)
Trouble concentrating	3 (quite a bit)
Feelings of worthlessness	3 (quite a bit)

development of the treatment plan proceeded as might be expected with depression (related to relationship problems) as the primary focus for treatment. They agreed to meet for eight sessions and then reevaluate the need for continuing treatment.

Dr. Z also asked Ms. Smith to complete the BSI prior to each session and gave her a brief rationale for the importance of the outcome assessment to track her progress and to assess her current levels of depression and thoughts of self-harm each week. Figure 6.1 displays Ms. Smith's scores over 14 sessions of treatment. As can be seen, Ms. Smith made relatively steady progress while she was in treatment. The session in which her scores increased (session 5) occurred the day after she and her partner had a serious argument. The final two sessions occurred at monthly intervals rather than the weekly interval of the earlier sessions. Although Ms. Smith did not resolve all her relationship issues while in treatment, both Ms. Smith and Dr. Z felt the treatment was successful.

Importantly, Ms. Smith's treatment was paid for by an insurance company that initially authorized eight sessions of treatment. When requesting authorization for additional treatment, Dr. Z faxed a copy of the tracking form completed up to the most recent session along with other clinical documentation. She indicated that Ms. Smith was making steady progress

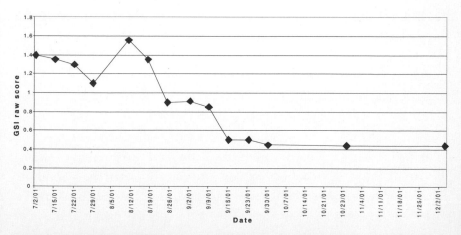

Figure 6.1 Tracking Chart for Ms. Smith Using the Global Severity Index of the Brief Symptom Inventory

as expected and that four to six additional sessions could be expected to result in improvement that would likely result in scores near the nonpatient average and be sufficient to indicate that Ms. Smith had significantly improved. Indeed, with a score of .44, Ms. Smith did eventually enter the recovered category using the BSI. A raw score of .44 was equivalent to a T-score of 37 when compared to women in outpatient treatment and a T-score of 56 when compared to nonpatient women.

EXAMPLE 2: CHILD CLIENT

Dr. E. Val Yuashun (henceforth Dr. Y) is a child clinical psychologist in a community mental health center. His work is primarily with families receiving outpatient treatment. The agency selected the Ohio Scales to assess all services for children and adolescents at the agency. During the implementation phase of the project, Dr. Y learned some potential methods for using the data and has integrated the outcome assessment data into his clinical routine.

All clients who enter treatment are asked by the receptionist to complete the Ohio Scales prior to their visit with an intake worker. If the identified child client is 12 or older, then the child completes the child form of the Ohio Scales and a parent or parent surrogate completes the parent form of the Ohio Scales. For children under 12, only the parent completes the forms. These scannable forms are then scanned, entered into a database, and used to produce brief reports with available data. The reports are then given to the clinician along with the other paperwork that needs to be completed during the intake interview. Following the interview and any other collection of collateral information, the intake worker is also asked to rate the youth using the agency-worker form of the Ohio Scales.

In many cases, the intake worker refers the family to another clinician. As a result, the initial treatment plan may be quite brief and the second clinician completes a more extensive treatment plan after reviewing the intake paperwork and visiting with the client. Although the parent and youth complete the problem severity, hopefulness, satisfaction, and functioning scales of the Ohio Scales, only the problem severity scores (agency worker, parent, and youth if applicable) are monitored using a tracking form in each client's chart. The following case illustrates Dr. Y's use of the data for a specific case.

Johnny Trubell is a 13-year-old youth who was referred by the school. He has been truant 5 days over the past 6 weeks and has received multiple in-school detentions as a result of disrespectful behavior, tardiness, and general disruption in class. J. T. lives with his mother and one younger half-sister. His father lives in the same community and has infrequent visits with J. T.

When Dr. Y is first referred the case, he reviews the intake paperwork. At the intake, J. T. and his mother, Brenda Trubell (henceforth Ms. T), completed respective forms of the Ohio Scales. J. T.'s total problem severity score of 20 fell in the mild range, while his mother's ratings of his problem behaviors produced a score of 35, which falls in the moderate range. J. T.'s score fell one standard deviation above the community comparison group; Ms. T's rating fell two and one half standard deviations above that mean and above the clinical cutoff score of 25. The intake worker rated J. T. as a 40 (moderate range).

Dr. Y first examines four critical items to identify any immediate risks that may need to be addressed—thoughts of death, self-harm, drug and alcohol use, and breaking the law. In addition, he asks whether any arguing or fighting leads to potential aggressiveness or other threats of physical harm to others. In J. T.'s case, only the breaking-the-law item is rated as a 1 (sometimes) by Ms. T. All the other critical items are rated 0 (not at all) by both J. T. and his mother. The intake worker rated J. T. as a 2 (several times) on the item concerning breaking the law item.

When examining the individual items to find potential targets for treatment, Dr. Y notices that Ms. T has rated J. T. as a 4 (most of the time) or 5 (all of the time) on five items—arguing, lying, skipping school, excessive activity, and self-criticism. In contrast, J. T. has much lower ratings on the same items. Dr. Y also notices that Ms. T and J. T. rated several items as high on the functioning scale (lower scores are more impairment on this scale)—self-care (e.g., hygiene), relationships with peers, recreation, and chores. These items may be indicative of strengths that might be used to support change in treatment.

Based on this data, Dr. Y meets with J. T. and Ms. T in their second session and they agree to begin treatment with intermittent family and individual sessions to help Ms. T develop skills for managing J. T.'s behavior and to help J. T. develop some impulse control and anger management skills. The difference between Ms. T and J. T.'s ratings on the forms is evident in the session as it becomes clear that J. T. views his behaviors as much less problematic than do Ms. T., the intake worker, and school personnel. As a result, a particular emphasis will be placed on helping Ms. T to develop effective parenting skills. In addition, there is also a need to help her develop a collaborative relationship with school personnel to get quicker feedback and to intervene more quickly in relationship to J. T.'s deteriorating school performance.

In this particular agency, outcome data are gathered every 3 months as part of the treatment plan update or at termination, whichever comes first. For many of the outpatient cases, only two outcome assessments are obtained—intake and a final session. In this particular case three data points are gathered—intake, 3 months, and termination at 5 months. A tracking graph is displayed in Figure 6.2. As is visible, only the agency worker rating is available at 5 months because J. T. and Ms. T dropped out of treatment when school ended and were not available to complete the final outcome assessment ratings. In addition, although the intake worker completed the

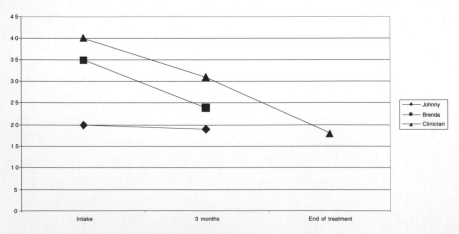

Figure 6.2 Change Over Time for J. T.

initial rating, Dr. Y completed the 3-month and 5-month ratings of J. T.'s progress.

As can be seen, J. T. made some apparent progress while enrolled in treatment from Dr. Y's point of view. His behavior change was less obvious over the first 3 months of treatment from Ms. T's point of view. J. T.'s own ratings suggested that he never really viewed his behavior as a serious problem in the first place and this view did not change much.

EXAMPLE 3: INDIVIDUAL AND AGGREGATE DATA ON AN INPATIENT UNIT

Dr. Anna Sesment (henceforth Dr. S) is a psychologist at a 20-bed acute inpatient care facility for adults. The majority of patients at the facility are committed to the hospital due to attempts or threats of harm to self or others, in combination with a bona fide psychiatric disorder. Dr. S is in charge of setting up a new system of measurement by which hospital staff can document patient progress throughout their stay in the hospital. The system should serve a twofold purpose in not only helping staff to determine when patients are making improvement, but also in helping to demonstrate the efficacy of the psychological and psychiatric interventions provided at the hospital upon a patient's release back into his or her place of residence.

Dr. S has decided that if the system is to be effective, all patients who are able to do so should complete an evaluation measure upon arrival at the hospital and at least once more during their stay at the hospital. This way, staff can have ample data (at least two data points) for each patient and patients will not have to bother completing the forms every day while in the facility. If the stay at the hospital is less than a week, which is possible given that the average stay at Dr. S's inpatient unit is between 5 and 6 days, then the assessment can be done when discharge occurs. Again, this decision would be based on patient behaviors; clients who appear to be improving by the third day of treatment and who are scheduled for release may be given the outcome measure at that time. Dr. S decided to use the Behavior and Symptom Identification Scale (BASIS-32) for the assessment of outcome with all patients receiving services in the inpatient unit, provided the patients are functioning well enough to complete the scale at intake. Dr. S selected this instrument primarily because it is a scale that has been used quite successfully in inpatient settings in the past. Furthermore, it is brief (32 items), and it provides an overall global measure that can be used for tracking change during a patient's stay; it also has five subscales, including an all-important psychosis subscale.

An added advantage of the BASIS-32 for Dr. S is that the makers of the instrument provide a performance measurement system for an additional cost. The system can help her evaluate program goals and outcome without spending precious clinical hours doing analyses. Data can be sent to the developers of the instrument and then analyses of data are returned to the hospital, providing Dr. S with important information about how the program is meeting its goals and how it stacks up against other similar programs. In addition, the data can be used as part of the requirements for Joint Commission accreditation.

Dr. S decided that each patient should complete the BASIS-32 as part of the initial paperwork during the hospital intake interview. The BASIS-32 was given to patients by intake specialists at the hospital when their intake forms were completed. The forms are then scored by the intake specialist and become part of the patient's hospital file. The file is then flagged so that data will be entered into a computer database along with minimal demographic information, and then it is submitted to the BASIS-32 analysis staff at McLean Hospital in Massachusetts. Although not of immediate importance for the treatment of individual patients, when enough data is collected and sent to be analyzed, patterns of treatment will emerge and can help determine the efficacy of treatment on the inpatient unit. BASIS-32 staff will provide a report that will be helpful in determining how the evaluation process is going and how patients at the unit fare in comparison to benchmarked norms. This information could be provided for payors, government agencies, and other relevant referral agencies for the hospital.

Along with a scored BASIS-32, a tracking sheet for each patient is also included in their hospital file. Thus, with each administration of the BASIS-32 (pre and post), the patient's overall score and subscale scores are included in the tracking form throughout the course of treatment. The data can be used to assist with the treatment planning and monitoring of treatment for each patient.

In order to demonstrate how individual data on the BASIS-32 can be used in inpatient treatment, let's consider the example of John Smith. Mr. Smith completed the BASIS-32 at intake and his scores, when compared to the normative data, were indicative of pathology overall and in the areas of relation to self/others and depression/anxiety. Intake data combined with other clinical assessment indicated that Mr. Smith met the criteria for depression and that he has been withdrawn and suicidal for the past few weeks, thus lending further evidence of the validity of data gathered by the BASIS-32. Information from the BASIS-32 confirmed the extent of these problems, and also tipped Dr. S off to some other problems: Mr. Smith endorsed item 23 (hearing voices) with a 2, indicating that he has had "moderate difficulty" with hearing voices in the past week. Thus, some psychotic symptoms are present with the depression, although not enough to elevate the overall psychoticism scale.

In addition, Dr. S performed an informal scan of the 32 scaled items looking for any that were endorsed as a 3 (quite a bit of difficulty) or 4 (extreme difficulty). Five items were endorsed as 3s or 4s. These items dealt with depression and a poor relation to self, further confirming the magnitude of his depressed mood.

During the initial treatment session after the interview, Dr. S briefly discussed the assessment results with Mr. Smith, including a discussion of the critical items, elevated scales, and his overall problem severity. Of course, self-harm was a central theme that Dr. S suggested should be revisited at every individual and group session with Mr. Smith during his stay at the hospital.

Dr. S was able to utilize the information from the intake evaluation and the BASIS-32 to formulate a treatment plan for Mr. Smith. It was decided that the harm to self, depressive symptoms, and hearing voices would be the targeted symptoms and that another administration would occur when he was ready for release. Both Dr. S and the psychiatrist on staff agreed that Mr. Smith should be held in the facility for at least 96 hours and then they would discuss his situation again.

Mr. Smith was asked to complete the BASIS-32 again on his fifth day on the unit after staff decided that his condition had stabilized and he should be eligible to return home that day. His overall BASIS-32 score was still slightly elevated, as was his anxiety/depression score, but he no longer had an elevated relation to self/others score. He also did not endorse item 23 (psychosis) or any of the self-harm questions as problems any longer. Clearly, Mr. Smith had made progress while in treatment and was no longer considered a danger to himself (or others) by hospital personnel. He was referred to outpatient counseling and outpatient psychiatry and agreed to continue taking a prescribed antidepressant.

Individually, the data from the BASIS-32 helped in Mr. Smith's treatment. On an aggregate level, the data were useful in helping establish treatment protocols for the hospital based on subscale and overall scores. The data Mr. Smith provided was combined with data gathered from every other inpatient at Dr. S's hospital from that fiscal year. Dr. S used the report from BASIS-32 to determine usual treatment protocols for patients with various score elevations. For example, patients who had elevated anxiety scores were referred to a special systematic desensitization group offered in the evenings at the hospital. Thus, special programs were conceived in order to fit the needs of patients with various profile elevations.

EXAMPLE 4: ADMINISTRATIVE DATA REGARDING THERAPISTS

In a relatively large counseling center serving the student body of a public university, the administration decided to institute a standardized system for outcome-data collection with the OQ-45 as the primary outcome assessment instrument. In addition to the OQ-45, the center administers post-service satisfaction questionnaires via a mailed survey. All students entering services complete the OQ-45 prior to the intake and each subsequent session. The data are scored and entered into a counseling center information system for further aggregate data analysis. The counseling center has one doctoral-level employee who is hired as a half-time clinician and half-time data analyst to conduct program evaluation and general outcome assessment. Certain reports are used internally for administrative decision making and other reports are generated to pass on to the upper administration to document service effectiveness and efficiency as well as to communicate the needs of the center in a clear and data-based manner.

As therapists are hired at the agency, they are informed about the data collection system and the possibility that client outcomes will be used to provide feedback to therapists at the end of each year. Client outcome data are not to be used for employment-related decisions, but may be used by the clinical director to inform potential training issues and other plans for individualized clinical development among the therapists; this is especially true for interns and students who provide services at the center. In this particular instance the data analyst is working with the center's clinical director, who will provide the feedback to the clinicians.

For this example, the 27 therapists who work in the counseling center (some interns and some full-time staff) are examined regarding their performance during the past year in terms of both client outcomes and satisfaction. Using the data from the past year, the data analyst takes every client seen by the 27 therapists and examines the difference between the first and last sessions. Clients who participated in fewer than three sessions (including the intake) were eliminated from the analysis. The remaining clients are then classified as recovered, unchanged, or deteriorated based on the size of the intake to last-session difference. Clients who make a 14-point change and who have an end-of-treatment score lower than 64 are classified as recovered. Clients who get worse by 14 points are classified as deteriorated. All other clients are classified as unchanged. The clients are then grouped within therapists and the percent of each therapists' case load that are recovered, unchanged, or deteriorated is calculated. In Table 6.3, the percentages and number of clients for each therapist are presented. The bottom row has the average percent recovered, unchanged, and deteriorated for the agency.

When looking at the current table, it is evident that several therapists have lower rates of clients who recover and higher rates of clients who are either unchanged or deteriorated. Notably, the number of clients per therapist differs substantially, with full-time therapists having much larger case-

Table 6.3 Therapist Rates of Client Recovery, No Change, and Deterioration

Therapist	% Recovered	% Unchanged	% Deteriorated	Number of Clients
1	40.0	52.0	8.0	25
2	31.3	62.4	6.3	16
3	30.5	60.3	9.2	141
4	36.7	53.3	10.0	60
5	23.7	63.1	13.2	38
6	19.2	80.8	0.0	52
7	38.5	53.8	7.7	26
8	30.9	59.5	9.6	94
9	14.0	70.0	16.0	50
10	28.6	66.6	4.8	21
11	0.0	60.0	40.0	5
12	20.0	63.6	15.9	44
13	28.0	63.0	8.2	73
14	24.1	67.5	8.4	83
15	30.6	59.7	9.7	62
16	31.3	62.4	6.3	16
17	20.0	66.7	13.3	15
18	41.7	41.6	16.7	24
19	37.0	48.2	14.8	27
20	27.8	63.9	8.3	36
21	37.2	58.1	4.7	43
22	26.2	59.5	14.3	42
23	27.5	58.0	14.5	69
24	64.7	31.5	4.8	17
25	30.8	61.5	7.7	13
26	37.0	55.6	7.4	54
27	28.6	57.1	14.3	7
Average	29.9	57.7	12.3	42.7

loads over the year than the interns and students. Satisfaction ratings were also examined by the data analyst and were uniformly positive for all therapists (on average) and represent approximately 14% of all clients served. As you will recall from earlier chapters, most satisfaction survey response rates are quite low and this was no exception.

These data were used to provide feedback to therapists in individual meetings with the center's clinical director, who gathered qualitative data regarding therapist caseloads and helped each therapist to develop a plan for continuing education and performance improvement for the coming year. With few exceptions, most therapists hovered around the agency means of approximately 12% of clients deteriorating and 30% reaching criteria for recovery. When using criteria for improvement instead of recovery (i.e., 14 points of change without considering the final end status—below 64), the rates are higher.

EXAMPLE 5: AGGREGATE REPORTING IN A PUBLIC AGENCY

In this example, data from a community mental health center that provides community support services to families with children who have serious emotional and behavioral disorders was collected to help demonstrate the effectiveness of publicly funded services. The following example report was created by the agencies' evaluator, who produced the report for the agency's board of directors and the state department of mental health. Information in brackets shows where specific details would normally be included in such a report.

This example illustrates the typical manner in which outcome data could be portrayed in a report to a nonprofit agency's board of directors or within a state-funded agency in a report to the state department of mental health. Of course, some states are developing statewide systems of collecting data. As a result, such reports may be redundant if the state already has the information. However, aggregate data can be quite useful for illustrating the level of severity of clients entering services, the rates of change or outcome of service for the average client, and level of satisfaction with services if such data are collected.

When agencies gather every-session data, the analyses will be even more informative because the rates of attrition will be much lower. Similarly, rates of service usage can then be reported (e.g., the average client attended six sessions of outpatient treatment). Service usage data, when combined with outcome and satisfaction data, can be quite impressive.

Report of Outcomes for Community Support Program

Introduction

The community support program has been gathering data regarding the effectiveness of its services over the past year. [Note: Insert other relevant information here.] This report presents a summary of findings regarding the initial status of clients entering services, the clinical outcome of services, and client satisfaction with services.

Data Collection

One hundred clients rated their outcomes using the [Note: Insert name of global child outcome measure here] every session while attending treatment. [Note: Insert other relevant demographic data (e.g., age range, gender, etc.) about the clients who receive services here.]

Measures

[Insert a brief description of the selected measure here.] The measure was administered to families entering treatment at their initial referral to the community support program and every 3 months thereafter during treatment. Both parents and youth rated their outcomes on respective forms.

Initial Status

The initial scores of the parents and youth give some indication of the severity of problems and level of functioning for youth entering outpatient services. The average initial score on each scale is listed in Table 1 alongside the relevant community comparison group score.

Table 1. Average Initial Scores

Rater/Scale	Intake X (SD)	Community X (SD)
Parent total	73.3 (17.8)	50 (10)
Youth total	63.3 (16.8)	50 (10)

Note: X = average score; SD = standard deviation

The scores in and of themselves are not useful unless compared to those of other youth. As a result, the average scores for a comparison sample are also presented. Clearly, the youth who are entering community support services have clinical levels of emotional and behavioral problems. Similarly, they have impaired functioning when compared to other youth in the community. [Note: The table could also be displayed graphically, include agency worker scores, or both.]

Clinical Outcome of Services

The families that agreed to participate in the study were asked to complete the outcome measure at intake and every three months thereafter while they were receiving services up to a one-year follow-up and at the end of services. [Note: Insert other relevant data about the outcome data collection.]

Table 2 displays the number of individuals who completed the forms at each time point. [Note: Insert other information about the reasons for continuing or dropping out of services.]

Table 2. Number of Individuals Completing the Follow-up Ratings

Rater	Intake	3 Months	6 Months	9 Months	12 Months
Parent	100	60	40	30	20
Youth	50	30	20	15	10

Although the number of dropouts was quite high, analyses were conducted to examine the perception of change in total scores for those who did continue. Paired T-tests examining changes from intake to 3 months were first examined. Means, standard deviations, and significance tests for the measures are presented in Table 3.

Table 3. Means, Standard Deviations, and Significance Tests for Two Sources of Information in Content Areas From Intake to 3-Month Assessment

Rater/Scale	Intake X (SD)	3 Months X (SD)	T	Sig.
Parent ($N = 60$) Total	73.3 (17.8)	58.0 (19.0)	3.64	.001
Youth ($N = 30$) Total	63.3 (16.8)	56.7 (21.2)	2.35	.057

As can be seen, the parents and youth reported significant changes on the total score. Figure 1 displays the change lines as rated by youth and parents while ignoring the drop out rates.

Figure 1 Change in Total Scores
[Note: Insert a figure depicting the change over time.]
[Note: Insert other graphs as appropriate for the data. A clinical significance graph may fit here too.]

Subscale Changes Rated by Parents and Youth
[Note: Similar description of changes in the subscales of the selected measure could be presented here with graphs and tables.]

Satisfaction With Services
In addition to rating clinical improvement over time, the parents and youth also rated their satisfaction with services. Figure 6.3 illustrates the satisfaction ratings for parents and youth on the eight satisfaction items. [Note: Each satisfaction item could be illustrated in a similar fashion here.]

As can be seen, parents were generally satisfied with services (100% somewhat, moderately, or extremely satisfied).
[Note: Insert a brief description of the graph for each of the eight items.]

Overall, these ratings suggest that the families who were receiving services were pleased with the services they received and felt that they were listened to and treated well as they participated in services.

Summary
Together the results of this report suggest that youth who participate in community support services have significant problems upon entering into the program. They make meaningful changes while participating in the program, especially when considering the total score on a global measure of change. Finally, they are generally satisfied with the services.

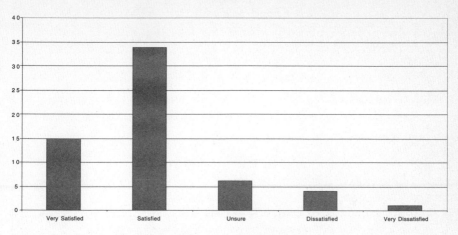

Figure 6.3 Parent Overall Satisfaction with Services

In our experience with conducting such analyses for agencies and programs, we have found that satisfaction data are almost always largely positive—that is, most clients are satisfied. As a result, the satisfaction data add a positive tone to any report on outcome data, which tend to be more conservative. Although clients on average will improve, when classified into recovered, unchanged, and deteriorated (as in the previous example) the rates are much lower and may be construed more negatively. This may be a function of the formulas for calculating rates of recovery. On the other hand, most clients entering treatment want to leave treatment with a clinical status that is similar to that of other individuals living in the community who have few psychological (either emotional or behavioral) symptoms. As a result, we recommend sticking with these conservative criteria that indicate return to the common conception of normal functioning.

🐟 TEST YOURSELF 🐟

1. **In the individual adult client case example, why was the Brief Symptom Inventory (BSI) chosen as the outcome measure?**

   (a) The BSI is the easiest instrument to score.

   (b) Her clients selected the BSI as their favorite outcome measure.

   (c) The norms have been shown to be valid.

   (d) The BSI has a global scale that can be used to track change in addition to other scales.

   (e) The BSI has several scales that can prove helpful in treatment planning.

2. **In the individual adult client case example, why did Dr. May Zurment ask about drug and alcohol abuse in addition to gathering BSI data?**

   (a) It is a requirement in her state to ask clients about substance abuse.

   (b) She would want to detoxify her client if substance abuse were a concern.

   (c) The BSI does not address substance abuse issues and she believes they are important.

   (d) The BSI has several substance abuse questions, but they are not well normed.

   (e) None of the above.

3. **In the child client case example, the child, Johnny Trubell, is 13 years old and the Ohio Scales were used as the outcome measure. At his age, who could participate in the completion of the Ohio Scales?**

   (a) Johnny, his mother, and the clinician, because Johnny is older than 11 years of age

   (b) Johnny's mother and the clinician, because Johnny is younger than 14 years of age

   (c) the clinicians only, because it is an intake

   (d) the parent only, because Johnny is too young to complete the forms

   (e) Johnny and his mother, because the clinician has just met Johnny

4. The evaluation revealed some trouble for Johnny in the area of breaking the law. Which of the following would best characterize that information?

(a) Global score

(b) Critical item

(c) Subscale score

(d) Target complaint

(e) Superfluous data

5. In the administrative data regarding therapists case example, client outcome was classified in terms of patients who

(a) recovered.

(b) were left unchanged.

(c) deteriorated.

(d) none of the above.

(e) all of the above.

6. In the administrative data regarding therapists case example, data was gathered for clients during every session, and for the purposes of classification, data was compared at what time periods?

(a) Every three sessions

(b) Every other session

(c) Intake and final session

(d) Intake and then every month thereafter

(e) Intake and then every 3 months thereafter

7. In the aggregate data case example, which of the following was information that can be obtained only by gathering data every session as opposed to specific time periods?

(a) Satisfaction data

(b) Service usage data

(c) Level of severity data

(d) Functioning data

(e) All of the above

(continued)

8. **In the adult inpatient case example, which of the following is the main reason Dr. Anna Sesment chose the Behavior and Symptom Identification Scale (BASIS-32)?**

   (a) Scores on the measures cannot be compared to benchmarked scores.

   (b) Scores on the measure can be used to formulate a treatment plan.

   (c) It is the only brief, user-friendly measure on the market.

   (d) It has been used quite successfully in inpatient settings.

   (e) The number 32 has long been Dr. Sesment's favorite number.

Answers: 1. d; 2. c; 3. a; 4. b; 5. e; 6. c; 7. b; 8. d

Seven

CONCLUSIONS

I n this brief exploration of the essentials of outcome assessment, we have attempted to arm the clinician with the basic tools that are necessary for conducting a realistic program of outcome assessment in a practice, group, or agency. Prefaced by a history of psychotherapy research that has demonstrated the efficacy and effectiveness of psychotherapy, modern methods of patient-oriented research can be used by the practitioner to evaluate his or her own practice. Although a variety of ways have been developed to conduct this assessment using individualized or standardized scales, our preference and focus throughout the book was the use of global client-report measures that could be administered before every session. These data can be useful for the individual client's treatment, and when aggregated, they can be useful for determining the overall success of the clinician, program, or agency. On a governmental level, these data could aid in the determination of what agencies, programs, or types of services are routinely effective, and could thus shape policy reform if deemed necessary.

On a much smaller but equally important scale, the individual client's treatment can benefit through the use of initial data to inform the treatment plan and for the identification of potential treatment issues. Critical items can be examined to alert the clinician regarding immediate risks, and treatment can be tailored in part based on the initial information gathered through the administration of an outcome instrument. Outcome instruments are not designed with detailed diagnostic assessment and personality description in mind, yet they provide some limited, useful information for treatment planning and for clinical intervention.

Although initial data to supplement the intake interview are useful, the primary reason for administering outcome measures during treatment is to track the change of the individual client. With every session administration, the clinician gains access to useful standardized data regarding client progress. These data can be gathered independent of practice (measurement), given to the clinician (monitored), or used by the clinician or others (e.g., supervisors, administrators, or payors) to manage the outcome of treatment through the potential modification of treatment. In addition, other data collection strategies aside from every-session data collection strategies may be used depending on the circumstances. Nevertheless, we have argued for every-session outcome collection in outpatient practice because of the potential problems with attrition and data collection mechanics that accompany other avenues of outcome assessment.

Particular emphasis has been given to the identification of failing cases and the potential utility of tracking the progress of clients who do not improve as expected. Indeed, the ability to identify and modify treatment in these cases may be the single most important use of data regarding client progress. It is well documented that approximately 10% of all clients who attend therapy not simply fail to make progress, but actually get worse while they are in treatment. If therapists can be informed about these cases and make modifications in treatment as necessary, the rates of success in psychotherapy can be substantially improved. One might argue that this 10% of clients may be the group who use the most resources and will require the best research in the future in order to benefit from treatment. The first step in this process is identifying the clients who do not improve as expected, and then the matter of appropriate, timely intervention is important.

Importantly, individual data can also be used for communicating with the insurance company or managed-care organization that is paying for the client's services. Accurate documentation of treatment accompanied by recognizable, standardized outcome measurement data can be quite compelling in negotiations for appropriate treatment. The data can help inform all concerned regarding the current amount of improvement or lack thereof and may be connected to other relevant treatment information (e.g., environmental events such as a death in the family). With solid data forming a foundation for treatment, the clinician is more likely to be viewed as credible by the payor and will be better informed regarding treatment for the clinician's own purposes.

When aggregated, outcome data can be used to help to inform internal users (e.g., supervisors, administrators, and nonprofit boards) and external users (private or public contracting agencies) regarding the success of the clinician, program, or agency. Although these uses require more statistical skills, basic methods of aggregating data can be used to examine the performance of a therapist, program, or agency. In addition, other analyses of outcome data may identify certain subgroups of clients who need additional or modified services. The data will help to select services or identify clients who may not progress to the degree expected or at a rate that is consistent with other clients who receive services. In short, treatment and programmatic decisions can be informed by the ongoing collection of outcome data. Clinicians should note that even without standardized outcome measures, decisions are still being made by administrators and policy planners about the efficacy of treatment in various programs and among specific clinicians. We are suggesting that data from solid outcome measures be used to help guide these decisions so that changes in treatment can be based on solid evidence rather than mere speculation.

Although outcome data are quite useful for tracking individual change and creating reports regarding the overall effectiveness of a clinician or program, the data are not experimental. As a result, the individual who creates the reports should be careful not to make causal attributions regarding the data, nor should they insinuate that the data are equivalent to those gathered in experimental settings with tight controls and random assignment. Clients may improve during treatment as a result of numerous external circumstances that are not in the control of the therapist or agency. Having methods of documenting that clients are achieving expected outcomes while in treatment is useful correlational data that suggests clients may be benefiting from treatment. However, such data are correlational, not experimental, and should not be viewed as direct evidence that treatment certainly works or caused the improvement. Should clinicians get the itch to say that these data are sufficient evidence that their therapy works, they must remember that in that case all clients who deteriorate must do so as a direct result of their treatment too! Furthermore, lasting change can only be documented by follow-up studies well after treatment, an undertaking that is far too costly in time and resources for most mental health care providers.

The correlational nature of outcome evaluation data may be limiting in some ways, but the data are also very useful in others. Consistent with their very purpose, the most important uses of outcome evaluation data revolve around the measurement, monitoring, and management of treatment for the individual client. These uses enhance the clinical processes and have a distinct possibility of improving the quality of treatment. As a result, we would not be surprised (and would in fact be delighted) if these methods gradually become more integrated into the payment processes of both private and public service systems. We hope that the methods of integrating outcome assessment into payment will be focused on quality service and not solely on finding the least costly services. Although cost is important, it should never come at the price of quality—but this is an issue for another book.

The use of data for examining the performance of therapists will be a controversial topic for the future. Undoubtedly, insurance companies and others who pay for or manage mental health services are already evaluating the performance of therapists using outcome data (e.g., satisfaction) or other process (e.g., treatment plans, length of time between referral and first appointment) and utilization (e.g., number of sessions) information. Certainly, the routine assessment of client outcomes will provide another source of information regarding therapist effectiveness. In addition, it is often practical to administer a simple client outcome measure. The use of a simple measure is also an important limitation of monitoring patient treatment response. Care must be taken to assure that such data are used fairly (e.g., via case-mix adjustment) and with due consideration for the many external events that may influence client outcome. Certainly, oncologists should not be judged solely on their rates of patient survival from cancer. Yet, if stricken with a potentially fatal variant of cancer, each of us might prefer to be seen by the physician who has the best success rates. Similar thought must be given to any data that are aggregated within clinicians so that outcome assessment does not become an unnecessary source of conflict, worry, or grief for clinicians.

In summary, we have provided some brief, simple, and useful methods for implementing an outcome evaluation process in practice. As we have mentioned throughout the book, these data may be used for a variety of purposes. However, the ball is now in the reader's court. The actual decisions regarding the implementation and use of outcome data in practice will be up to each individual clinician, program, and agency. For those who embark down the outcome path, we wish you well and welcome your feedback regarding the utility of this primer. For those who wait, we'll try to persuade you via other publications. The age of accountability can be seen as an invitation to improve the quality of care for all those clients who put their trust in the providers who strive to help them.

References

Achenbach, T. M. (1999). The Child Behavior Checklist and related instruments. In M. E. Maruish (Ed.), *The use of psychological testing for treatment planning and outcomes assessment* (2nd ed., pp. 429–466). Mahwah, NJ: Erlbaum.

Achenbach, T. M. (1991). *Manual for the Child Behavior Checklist/4–18 and 1991 Profile.* Burlington, VT: Department of Psychiatry, University of Vermont.

Achenbach, T. M., & Edelbrock, C. S. (1983). *Manual for the Child Behavior Checklist and Revised Child Behavior Profile.* Burlington, VT: Department of Psychiatry, University of Vermont.

Achenbach, T. M., McConaughty, S. H., & Howell, C. T. (1987). Child/adolescent behavioral and emotional problems: Implications of cross-informant correlations for situational specificity. *Psychological Bulletin, 101,* 213–232.

Anastasi, A. (1988). *Psychological testing* (6th ed.). New York: Macmillan.

Anderson, E. M., & Lambert, M. J. (1995). Short-term dynamically oriented psychotherapy: A review and meta-analysis. *Clinical Psychology Review, 15,* 503–514.

Anderson, E. M., & Lambert, M. J. (2001). A survival analysis of clinically significant change in outpatient psychotherapy. *Journal of Clinical Psychology, 57,* 875–888.

Andrews, G. (1995). Best practices in implementing outcome management: More science, more art, worldwide. *Behavioral Healthcare Tomorrow, 4,* 19–24.

Asay, T. P., Lambert, M. J., Gregersen, A. T., & Goates, M. K. (in press). Using patient-focused research in evaluating treatment outcome in private practice. *Journal of Clinical Psychology.*

Barkham, M., Evans, C., Margison, F., McGrath, G., Mellor-Clark, J., Milne, D., & Connell, J. (1998). The rational for developing and implementing core outcome batteries for routine use in service settings and psychotherapy outcome research. *Journal of Mental Health, 7,* 35–47.

Barkham, M., Leach, C., Lucock, M., Evans, C., Margison, F., Mellor-Clark, J., Benson, L., Connell, J., Audin, K., & McGrath, G. (2001). Service profiling and outcomes benchmarking using the CORE-OM: Toward practice-based evidence in the psychological therapies. *Journal of Consulting and Clinical Psychology, 69,* 184–196.

Barkham, M., Rees, A., Stiles, W. B., Shapiro, D. A., Hardy, G. E., & Reynolds, S. (1996). Dose effect relations in time limited psychotherapy for depression. *Journal of Consulting and Clinical Psychology, 64,* 927–935.

Barlow, D. H. (1981). On the relation of clinical research to clinical practice: Current issues, new directions. *Journal of Consulting and Clinical Psychology, 49,* 147–155.

Barlow, D. H., Hayes, S. C., & Nelson, R. O. (1984). *The scientist-practitioner: Research and accountability in clinical and educational settings.* New York: Pergamon.

Bartlett, J., & Cohen, J. (1993). Building an accountable, improvable delivery system. *Administration and Policy in Mental Health, 14,* 51–58.

Battle, C. C., Imber, S. D., Hoehn-Saric, R., Stone, A. R., Nash, E. H., & Frank, J. D. (1966). Target complaints as a criteria of improvement. *American Journal of Psychotherapy, 20,* 184–192.

Beck, A. T., Steer, R. A., & Garbin, M. G. (1988). Psychometric properties of the Beck Depression Inventory: Twenty-five years of evaluation. *Clinical Psychology Review, 8,* 77–100.

Beck, A. T., Ward, C. H., Mendelson, M., Mock, J., & Erbaugh, J. (1961). An inventory for measuring depression. *Archives of General Psychiatry, 4,* 561–571.

Bergin, A. E. (1971). The evaluation of therapeutic outcomes. In S. L. Garfield & A. E. Bergin (Eds.), *Handbook of psychotherapy and behavior change* (pp. 217–270). New York: Wiley.

Bernard, J. M., & Goodyear, R. K. (1992). *Fundamentals of clinical supervision.* Boston: Allyn & Bacon.

Beutler, L. E., Machado, P. P., & Neufeldt, S. A. (1994). Therapist variables. In A. E. Bergin & S. L. Garfield (Eds.), *Handbook of psychotherapy and behavior change* (4th ed., pp. 229–69). New York: Wiley.

Blanchard, E. B., & Schwarz, S. P. (1988). Clinically significant changes in behavioral medicine. *Behavioral Assessment, 10,* 171–188.

Bloom, M. & Fischer, J. (1982). *Evaluating practice: Guidelines for the accountable professional.* Englewood Cliffs, NJ: Prentice-Hall.

Breslin, F., Sobell, L. C., Buchan, G., & Cunningham, J. (1997). Toward a stepped-care approach to treating problem drinkers: The predictive validity of within-treatment variables and therapist prognostic ratings. *Addiction, 92*(11), 1479–1489.

Brown, G. S., Burlingame, G. M., Lambert, M. J., Jones, E., & Vaccaro, J. (2001). Pushing the quality envelope: A new outcomes management system. *Psychiatric Services, 52,* 925–934.

Brown, J., Dreis, S., & Nace, D. K. (1999). What really makes a difference in psychotherapy outcome? Why does managed care want to know? In M. A. Hubble & B. L. Duncan (Eds.), *The heart and soul of change: What works in therapy* (pp. 389–406). Washington, DC: American Psychological Association.

Brown, G. A., & Lambert, M. J. (June, 1998). Tracking patient progress: Decision making for cases who are not benefiting from psychotherapy. Paper presented at the Annual Meeting of the Society for Psychotherapy Research. Snowbird, UT.

Bryk, A. S., & Raudenbush, S. W. (1992). *Hierarchical linear models: Applications and data analysis methods.* Newbury Park, CA: Sage.

Bryk, A. S., Raudenbush, S. W., & Congdon, R. T. (1996). HLM for Windows (Version 4.01.01) [Computer Software]. Lincolnwood, IL: SSI, Inc.

Burchard, J. D., & Schaefer, M. (1992). Improving accountability in a service delivery system in children's mental health. *Clinical Psychology Review, 12,* 867–882.

Burlingame, G. M., Wells, M. G., & Lambert, M. J. (1996). *Youth Outcome Questionnaire.* Stevenson, MD: American Professional Credentialing Services.

Callaghan, G. (2001). Demonstrating clinical effectiveness for individual practitioners and clinics. *Professional Psychology: Research & Practice, 32,* 289–297.

Calsyn, R. J., & Davidson, W. S. (1978). Do we really want a program evaluation strategy based on individualized goals? A critique of goal attainment scaling. *Evaluation Studies: Review Annual, 1,* 700–713.

Ciarlo, J. A., Brown, T. R., Edwards, D. W., Kiresuk, T. J., & Newman, F. L. (1986). *Assessing mental health treatment outcome measurement techniques* (DHHS Publication No. ADM 86-1301). Washington, DC: U.S. Government Printing Office.

Clement, P. W. (1996). Evaluation in private practice. *Clinical Psychology: Science and Practice, 3,* 146–159.

Clement, P. W. (1999). *Outcome and incomes.* New York: Guilford.

Cobb, J. P., Mathews, A. M., Childs-Clarke, A., & Blowers, C. M. (1984). The spouse as co-therapist in the treatment of agoraphobia. *British Journal of Psychiatry, 144,* 282–287.

Cone, J. D. (2001). *Evaluating outcomes: Empirical tools for effective practice.* Washington, DC: American Psychological Association.

Corcoran, K., & Fischer, J. (1987). *Measures for clinical practice.* New York: The Free Press.

Cross, T. P., McDonald, E., & Lyons, H. (1997). Evaluating the outcome of children's mental health services: A guide for the use of available child and family outcome measures (2nd ed.). Boston: Judge Baker Children's Center.

Davis, R. D., Meagher, S. E., Goncalves, A., Woodward, M., & Millon, T. (1999). Treatment planning and outcome in adults: The Millon Clinical Multiaxial Inventory–III. In M. E. Maruish (Ed.), *The use of psychological testing for treatment planning and outcomes assessment* (2nd ed., pp. 1051–1081). Mahwah, NJ: Erlbaum.

Derogatis, L. R. (1993). *BSI: Administration, scoring, and procedures manual* (3rd ed.). Minneapolis, MN: National Computer Systems.

Derogatis, L. R. (1994). *SCL-90-R: Administration, scoring, and procedures manual.* Minneapolis, MN: National Computer Systems.

Derogatis, L. R. (1983). SCL-90: Administration, scoring, and procedures manual for the revised version. Baltimore: Clinical Psychometric Research.

Derogatis, L. R., & Melisaratos, N. (1983). The Brief Symptom Inventory: An introductory report. *Psychological Medicine, 13,* 595–605.

Dorwart, R. A., Adler, D. A., Berlant, J. L., Dixon, L. B., Docherty, J. P., Ellison, J. M., Goldman, H. H., Sageman, M., & Siris, S. G. (1996). Outcomes management strategies in mental health: Application and implications for clinical practice. In L. I. Sederer & B. Dickey (Eds.) *Outcome assessment in clinical practice (pp. 45–54).* Baltimore: Williams & Wilkins.

Eisen, S. V., & Culhane, M. A. (1999). Behavior and Symptom Identification Scale. In M. E. Maruish (Ed.), *The use of psychological testing for treatment planning and outcomes assessment* (2nd ed., pp. 759–790). Mahwah, NJ: Erlbaum.

Eisen, S. V., Dill, D. L., & Grob, M. C. (1994). Reliability and validity of a brief patient-report instrument for psychiatric outcome evaluation. *Hospital and Community Psychiatry, 45,* 242–247.

Eisen, S. V., Grob, M. C., & Klein, A. A. (1986). BASIS: The development of a self-report measure for psychiatric inpatient evaluation. *The Psychiatric Hospital, 17,* 165–171.

Eisen, S. V., & Dickey, B. (1996). Mental health outcome assessment: The new agenda. *Psychotherapy, 33,* 181–189.

Eisen, S. V., Leff, H. S., & Shaefer, E. (1999). Implementing outcome systems: Lessons from a test of the BASIS-32 and the SF-36. *Journal of Behavioral Health Services & Research, 26,* 18–27.

Emmelkamp, P. M. G., Kuipers, A. C. M., & Eggeraat, J. B. (1978). Cognitive modification versus prolonged exposure in vivo: A comparison with agoraphobic subjects. *Behavior Research and Therapy, 16,* 33–41.

Eysenck, H. J. (1952). The effects of psychotherapy: An evaluation. *Journal of Consulting Psychology, 16,* 319–324.

Finch, A. E., Lambert, M. J., & Schaalje, B. G. (2001). Psychotherapy quality control: The statistical generation of expected recovery curves for integration into an early warning system. *Clinical Psychology and Psychotherapy, 8,* 231–42.

Fischer, J., & Corocran, K. (1994). Measures for clinical practice: A sourcebook (2nd ed.). New York: The Free Press.

Froyd, J., Lambert, M. J., & Froyd, J. (1996). A review of practices of psychotherapy outcome measurement. *Journal of Mental Health (UK), 5,* 11–15.

Garfield, S. L. (1994). Research on client variables in psychotherapy. In A. E. Bergin & S. L. Garfield (Eds.), *Handbook of psychotherapy and behavior change* (4th ed., pp. 190–228). New York: Wiley.

Gelso, C. J. (1979). Research in counseling: Methodological and professional issues. *The Counseling Psychologist, 8,* 7–35.

Gregersen, A. T., Nielsen, S. L., Isakson, R. L., Lambert, M. J., Smart, D. W., & Worthen, V. E. (August, 2001). Recalling and estimating emotional states: Are consumer reports accurate? Poster presented at the 109th Annual Conference of the American Psychological Association, San Francisco, CA.

Gregory, R. J. (1996). Psychological testing: History, principles, and applications. Boston: Allyn & Bacon.

Gregory, R. J. (1987). *Adult intellectual assessment.* Boston: Allyn & Bacon.

Haas, E., Hill, R., Lambert, M. J., & Morrell, B. (in press). Unraveling the early response mystery: Do early responders maintain treatment gains? *Journal of Clinical Psychology.*

Hansen, N. B., Lambert, M. J., & Forman, E. M. (in press). The psychotherapy dose-response effect and its implications for treatment delivery services. *Clinical Psychology: Research and Practice.*

Hawkins, R. P., Mathews, J. R., & Hamdan, L. (1999). *Measuring behavioral health outcomes: A practical guide.* New York: Plenum.

Hodges, K., & Wong, M. M. (1996). Psychometric characteristics of a multidimensional measure to assess impairment: The Child and Adolescent Functional Assessment Scale. *Journal of Child and Family Studies, 5,* 445–467.

Horowitz, L. M., Rosenberg, S. E., Baer, B. A., Ureno, G., & Villesenor, V. S. (1988). Inventory of Interpersonal Problems: Psychometric properties and clinical applications. *Journal of Consulting and Clinical Psychology, 56,* 885–892.

Howard, K. I., Kopta, S. M., Krause, M. S., & Orlinsky, D. E. (1986). The dose-effect relationship in psychotherapy. *American Psychologist, 41,* 159–164.

Howard, K. I., Moras, K. B., Brill, P. L., Martinovich, Z., & Lutz, W. (1996). Evaluation of psychotherapy: Efficacy, effectiveness, and patient progress. *American Psychologist, 51,* 1059–1064.

Ihilevich, D., & Gleser, G. C. (1982). *Evaluating mental-health programs: The Progress Evaluation Scales.* Lexington, MS: D. C. Heath and Company.

Jacobson, N. S., & Revenstorf, D. (1988). Statistics for assessing the clinical significance of psychotherapy techniques: Issues, problems, and new developments. *Behavioral Assessment, 10,* 133–145.

Jacobson, N. S., & Truax, P. (1991). Clinical significance: A statistical approach to defining meaningful change in psychotherapy research. *Journal of Consulting and Clinical Psychology, 59,* 12–19.

Jacobson, N. S., Follette, W. C., & Revenstorf, D. (1984). Psychotherapy outcome research: Methods for reporting variability and evaluating clinical significance. *Behavior Therapy, 15,* 336–352.

Jacobson, N. S., Roberts, L. J., Berns, S. B., & McGlinchey, J. B. (1999). Methods for defining and determining the clinical significance of treatment effects: Description, application, and alternatives. *Journal of Consulting and Clinical Psychology, 67,* 300–307.

Joint Commission on Accreditation of Healthcare Organizations. (1994). *A guide to establishing programs for assessing outcomes in clinical settings.* Oakbrook Terrace, IL: Author.

Kadera, S. W., Lambert, M. J., & Andrews, A. A. (1996). How much therapy is really enough? A session-by-session analysis of the psychotherapy dose-effect relationship. *Psychotherapy: Research and Practice, 5,* 1–21.

Katz, R., Katz, J., & Shaw, B. F. (1999). Beck Depression Inventory and Hopelessness Scale. In M. E. Maruish (Ed.), *The use of psychological testing for treatment planning and outcomes assessment* (2nd ed., pp. 921–934). Mahwah, NJ: Erlbaum.

Kazak, A. E., Jarmas, A., & Snitzer, L. (1988). The assessment of marital satisfaction: An evaluation of the Dyadic Adjustment Scale. *Journal of Family Psychology, 2,* 82–91.

Kazdin, A. E. (1993). Evaluation in clinical practice: Clinically sensitive and systematic methods of treatment delivery. *Behavior Therapy, 24,* 11–45.

Kendall, P. C., & Grove, W. M. (1988). Normative comparisons in therapy outcome. *Behavioral Assessment, 10,* 147–158.

Kendall, P. C., Marrs-Garcia, A., Nath, S. R., & Sheldrick, R. C. (1999). Normative comparisons for the evaluation of clinical significance. *Journal of Consulting and Clinical Psychology, 67,* 285–299.

Kiresuk, T. J., & Sherman, R. E. (1968). Goal Attainment scaling: A general method for evaluating comprehensive community mental health programs. *Community Mental Health Journal, 4,* 443–452.

Kiresuk, T. J., Smith, A., & Cardillo, J. E. (Eds.). (1994). *Goal attainment scaling: Applications, theory, and measurement.* Hillsdale, NJ: Erlbaum.

Koch, J. R., Lewis, A., & McCall, D. (1998). A multistakeholder-driven model for developing an outcome management system. *Journal of Behavioral Health Services and Research, 25,* 151–162.

Kolb, L. C. (1977). *Modern clinical psychiatry.* Philadelphia: W. B. Saunders.

Kordy, H., Hannöver, W., & Richard, M. (2001). Computer assisted feedback driven active quality management for psychotherapy provision: The Stuttgart-Heidelberg model. *Journal of Consulting and Clinical Psychology, 69,* 173–183.

Lambert, M. J. (1983). Introduction to assessment of psychotherapy outcome: Historical perspective and current issues. In M. J. Lambert, E. R. Christensen, & S. S. DeJulio (Eds.), *The assessment of psychotherapy outcome* (pp. 3–32). New York: Wiley.

Lambert, M. J. (2001). Psychotherapy outcome and quality improvement: Introduction to the special section on patient-focused research. *Journal of Consulting and Clinical Psychology, 69,* 147–149.

Lambert, M. J., & Bergin, A. E. (1994). The effectiveness of psychotherapy. In A. E. Bergin & S. L. Garfield (Eds.), *Handbook of psychotherapy and behavior change* (4th ed., pp. 143–189). New York: Wiley.

Lambert, M. J., & Hawkins, E. J. (2001). Using information about patient progress in supervision: Are outcomes enhanced? *Australian Journal of Psychology, 36,* 131–138.

Lambert, M. J., & Hill, C. E. (1994). Assessing psychotherapy outcomes and processes. In A. E. Bergin & S. L. Garfield (Eds.), *Handbook of psychotherapy and behavior change* (4th ed., pp. 72–113). New York: Wiley.

Lambert, M. J., & Okiishi, J. C. (1997). The effects of the individual psychotherapist and implications for future research. *Clinical Psychology: Research and Practice, 4,* 66–75.

Lambert, M. J., & Brown, G. S. (1996). Data-based management for tracking outcome in private practice. *Clinical Psychology: Science and Practice, 14,* 172–178.

Lambert, M. J., & Finch, A. E. (1999). The Outcome Questionnaire. In M. E. Maruish (Ed.), *The use of psychological testing for treatment planning and outcomes assessment* (2nd ed., pp. 831–869). Mahwah, NJ: Erlbaum.

Lambert, M. J., & Ogles, B. M. (1997). The effectiveness of psychotherapy supervision. In C. E. Watkins (Ed.), *Handbook of psychotherapy supervision* (pp. 421–446). New York: Wiley.

Lambert, M. J., & Ogles, B. M. (in press). The efficacy and effectiveness of psychotherapy. In M. J. Lambert (Ed.), *Handbook of psychotherapy and behavior change* (5th ed.). New York: Wiley.

Lambert, M. J., Burlingame, G. M., Umphress, V., Hansen, N. B., Yancher, S. C., Vermeersch, D., & Clouse, G. C. (1996). The reliability and validity of a new psychotherapy outcome questionnaire. *Clinical Psychology and Psychotherapy, 3*(4), 249–258.

Lambert, M. J., Christensen, E. R., & DeJulio, S. S. (1983). *The assessment of psychotherapy outcome.* New York: Wiley.

Lambert, M. J., Hansen, N. B., & Finch, A. E. (2001). Patient-focused research: Using patient outcome data to enhance treatment effects. *Journal of Consulting and Clinical Psychology, 69,* 159–172.

Lambert, M. J., Hansen, N. B., Umphress, V., Lunnen, K., Okiishi, J., Burlingame, G., Huefner, J. C., & Reisinger, C. W. (1996). *Administration and scoring manual for the Outcome Questionnaire (OQ 45.2).* Wilmington, DE: American Professional Credentialing Services.

Lambert, M. J., Heufner, J. C., & Reisinger, C. W. (2000). Quality improvement: Current research in outcome management. In G. Stricker, W. G. Troy, & S. A. Shueman (Eds.), *Handbook of quality management in behavioral health* (pp. 95–110). New York: Kluwer Academic/Plenum.

Lambert, M. J., Masters, K. S., & Ogles, B. M. (1991). Outcome research in counseling. In C. E. Watkins & L. J. Schneider (Eds.), *Research in counseling* (pp. 51–83). Hillsdale, NJ: Erlbaum.

Lambert, M. J., Ogles, B. M., & Masters, K. S. (1992). Choosing outcome assessment devices: An organizational and conceptual scheme. *Journal of Counseling and Development, 70,* 527–532.

Lambert, M. J., Okiishi, J. C., Finch, A. E., & Johnson, L. D. (1998). Outcome assessment: From conceptualization to implementation. *Professional Psychology: Research and Practice, 29,* 63–70.

Lambert, M. J., Whipple, J. L., Smart, D. W., Vermeersch, D. A., Nielsen, S. L., & Hawkins, E. J. (2001). The effects of providing therapists with feedback on patient progress during psychotherapy: Are outcomes enhanced? *Psychotherapy Research, 11*(1), 49–68.

Lambert, M. J., Whipple, J. L., Vermeersch, D. A., Smart, D. W., Hawkins, E. J., Nielsen, L. S., & Goates, M. (in press). Providing therapists with feedback on patient progress as a method of enhancing psychotherapy outcomes: A replication. *Clinical Psychology and Psychotherapy.*

Lambert, M. J., Whipple, J. L., Bishop, M., Vermeersch, D. A., Gray, G. V., & Finch, A. E. (in press). Comparison of rationally and statistically derived recovery curves for improving the quality of patient care. *Clinical Psychology and Psychotherapy.*

Leuger, R. J., Howard, K. I., Martinovich, Z., Lutz, W., Anderson, E. E., & Grissom, G. (2001). Assessing treatment progress with individualized models of expected response. *Journal of Consulting and Clinical Psychology, 69,* 150–158.

Lick, J. (1973). Statistical vs. clinical significance in research on the outcome of psychotherapy. *International Journal of Mental Health, 2,* 26–37.

Luborsky, L., Singer, B., & Luborsky, L. (1975). Comparative outcome studies of psychotherapies. *Archives of General Psychiatry, 32,* 995–1008.

Lueger, R. J., Howard, K. I., Martinovitch, Z., Lutz, W., Andersen, E. E., & Grissom, G. (2000). Assessing treatment progress with individualized models of expected response. *Journal of Consulting and Clinical Psychology, 69,* 150–158.

Lunnen, K. M., & Ogles, B. M. (1998). A multi-perspective, multi-variable evaluation of reliable change. *Journal of Consulting and Clinical Psychology, 66,* 400–410.

Lyons, J. S., Howard, K. I., O'Mahoney, M. T., & Lish, J. D. (1997). *The measurement and management of clinical outcomes in mental health.* New York: Wiley.

Marks, I. M., & Mathews, A. M. (1978). Brief standard self-rating for phobic patients. *Behavior Research and Therapy, 17,* 263–267.

Marques, C. (1998). Manual-based treatment and clinical practice. *Clinical Psychology: Science & Practice, 5,* 400–402.

Maruish, M. E. (Ed.). (1999). The use of psychological testing for treatment planning and outcomes assessment (2nd ed.). Mahwah, NJ: Erlbaum.

Mathews, A. M., Gelder, M. G., & Johnston, D. W. (1981). *Agoraphobia: Nature and treatment.* New York: Guilford.

McGlynn, E. A. (1996). Domains of study and methodological challenges. In L. I. Sederer & B. Dickey (Eds.), *Outcomes assessment in clinical practice* (pp. 19–24). Baltimore: Williams & Wilkins.

Meier, S. T., & Davis, S. R. (1990). Trends in reporting psychometric properties of scales used in counseling psychology research. *Journal of Counseling Psychology, 37,* 113–115.

Meier, S. T., & Letsch, E. A. (2000). What is necessary and sufficient information for outcome assessment? *Professional Psychology: Research and Practice, 31,* 409–411.

Mental health: Does therapy help? (1995, November). *Consumer Reports, 60,* 734–739.

Meyer, F., & Schulte, D. (in press). Zur Validität der Beurteilung des des Theapieerfolgs durch Therapeuten [The validity of therapist ratings of therapy outcome]. *Zeitschrift für Klinishe Psychologie und Psychotherapie.*

Miller, R. C., & Berman, J. S. (1983). The efficacy of cognitive behavior therapies: A quantitative review of the research evidence. *Psychological Bulletin, 94,* 39–53.

Mintz, J., & Kiesler, D. J. (1982). Individualized measures of psychotherapy outcome. In P. C. Kendall & J. N. Butcher (Eds.), *Handbook of research methods in clinical psychology* (pp. 491–534). New York: Wiley.

Mizes, J. S., & Crawford, J. (1986). Normative values on the Marks and Mathews Fear Questionnaire: A comparison as a function of age and sex. *Journal of Psychopathology and Behavioral Assessment, 8,* 253–262.

Mohr, D. C. (1995). Negative outcome in psychotherapy: A critical review. *Clinical Psychology: Science and Practice, 2,* 1–27.

Mordock, J. B. (2000). Outcome assessment: Suggestions for agency practice. *Child Welfare, LXXIX,* 689–710.

Mueller, R., Lambert, M. J., & Burlingame, G. (1998). The Outcome Questionnaire: A confirmatory factor analysis. *Journal of Personality Assessment, 70,* 248–262.

Newman, F. L., Ciarlo, J. A., & Carpenter, D. (1999). Guidelines for selecting psychological instruments for treatment planning and outcome assessment. In M. E.

Maruish (Ed.), *The use of psychological testing for treatment planning and outcomes assessment* (2nd ed., pp. 153–170). Mahwah, NJ: Erlbaum.

Nietzel, M. T., & Trull, T. J. (1988). Meta-analytic approaches to social comparisons: A method for measuring clinical significance. *Behavioral Assessment, 10,* 159–169.

Nietzel, M. T., Russell, R. L., Hemmings, K. A., & Gretter, M. L. (1987). The clinical significance of psychotherapy for unipolar depression: A meta-analytic approach to social comparison. *Journal of Consulting and Clinical Psychology, 55,* 156–161.

Nunnaly, J. C. (1978). *Psychometric theory.* New York: Mcgraw-Hill.

Oei, F. P. S., Moylan, A., & Evans, L. (1991). Validity and clinical utility of the Fear Questionnaire for anxiety-disorder patients. *Psychological Assessment, 3,* 391–397.

Ogles, B. M., & Lambert, M. J. (1989). A meta-analytic comparison of twelve agoraphobia outcome instruments. *Phobia Practice and Research Journal, 2,* 115–125.

Ogles, B. M., Lambert, M. J., & Masters, K. S. (1996). *Assessing outcome in clinical practice.* Boston: Allyn & Bacon.

Ogles, B. M., Lambert, M. J., Weight, D. G., & Payne, I. R. (1990). Agoraphobia outcome measurement: A review and meta-analysis. *Psychological Assessment: A Journal of Consulting and Clinical Psychology, 2,* 317–325.

Ogles, B. M., & Lunnen, K. M. (1996). Assessing outcome in practice. *Journal of Mental Health, 5,* 35–46.

Ogles, B. M., Lunnen, K. M., & Bonesteel, K. (2001). Clinical significance: History, application, and current practice. *Clinical Psychology Review, 21,* 421–446.

Ogles, B. M., Melendez, G., Davis, D. C., & Lunnen, K. M. (2001). The Ohio Scales: Practical outcome assessment. *Journal of Child and Family Studies, 10,* 199–212.

Ohio Department of Mental Health. (2000). *The Ohio mental health client outcomes system: Procedural manual.* Columbus, OH: Author.

Okiishi, J., Ogles, B. M., & Lambert, M. J. (2000, June). *Waiting for supershrink: An empirical analysis of individual therapist effects.* Paper presented at the Society for Psychotherapy Research Conference, Chicago.

Oliver, L. W., & Spokane, A. R. (1988). Career intervention outcome: What contributes to client gain? *Journal of Counseling Psychology, 35,* 447–462.

Orlinsky, D. E., & Howard, K. I. (1980). Gender and psychotherapeutic outcome. In A. M. Brodsky & R. T. Hare-Mustin (Eds.), *Women in psychotherapy* (pp. 3–34). New York: Guilford.

Piotrowski, C., & Keller, J. W. (1989). Psychological testing in outpatient mental health facilities: A national study. *Professional Psychology: Research and Practice, 20,* 423–425.

Plante, T. G., Couchman, C. E., & Hoffman, C. A. (1998). Measuring treatment outcome and client satisfaction among children and families: A case report. *Professional Psychology: Research and Practice, 29,* 52–55.

Richard, M., & Kordy, H. (in press). Early treatment response: Conceptualization, predictive validity and application in quality management. *Zeitschrift fur Klinische Psychologie und Psychotherapie.*

Rosenblatt, A., & Attkisson, C. C. (1993). Assessing outcomes for sufferers of severe mental disorder: A conceptual framework and review. *Evaluation and Program Planning, 16,* 347–363.

Roth, A., & Fonagy, P. (1996). *What works for whom? A critical review of psychotherapy research.* New York: Guilford.

Schutte, N. S., & Malouff, J. M. (1995). *Sourcebook of adult assessment strategies.* New York: Plenum.

Sederer, L. I., & Dickey, B. (Eds.). (1996). *Outcomes assessment in clinical practice.* Baltimore: Williams & Wilkins.

Seligman, M. E. P. (1995). The effectiveness of psychotherapy: The Consumer Reports study. *American Psychologist, 50,* 965–974.

Smith, G. R., Fischer, E. P., Nordquist, C. R., Mosley, C. L., & Ledbetter, N. S. (1997). Implementing outcomes management systems in mental health settings. *Psychiatric Services, 48,* 364–368.

Smith, M. L., Glass, G. V., & Miller, T. I. (1980). *The benefits of psychotherapy.* Baltimore: Johns Hopkins University Press.

Spanier, G. B. (1976). Measuring dyadic adjustment: New scales for assessing the quality of marriage and similar dyads. *Journal of Marriage and the Family, 38,* 15–28.

Spanier, G. B., & Thompson, L. (1982). A confirmatory analysis of the Dyadic Adjustment Scale. *Journal of Marriage and the Family, 44,* 813–823.

Speer, D. C. (1998). *Mental health outcome evaluation.* San Diego, CA: Academic Press.

Speilberger, C. D., Gorusch, R. L., & Luchene, R. E. (1970). *Manual for the State-Trait Anxiety Inventory.* Palo Alto, CA: Consulting Psychologists Press.

Spielberger, C. D., Sydeman, S. J., Owen, A. E., & Marsh, B. J. (1999). Measuring anxiety and anger with the State-Trait Anxiety Inventory (STAI) and the State-Trait Anger Expression Inventory (STAXI). In M. E. Maruish (Ed.), *The use of psychological testing for treatment planning and outcomes assessment* (2nd ed., pp. 993–1021). Mahwah, NJ: Erlbaum.

Spielberger, C. D. (1983). *Manual for the State-Trait Anxiety Inventory STAI (Form Y).* Palo Alto, CA: Consulting Psychologists Press.

Stoltenberg, C. D., & Delworth, U. (1987). *Supervising counselors and therapists: A developmental approach.* San Francisco: Jossey-Bass.

Strupp, H. H., & Hadley, S. W. (1977). A tripartite model of mental health and therapeutic outcome: With special reference to negative effects in psychotherapy. *American Psychologist, 32,* 187–196.

Strupp, H. H., Horowitz, L. M., & Lambert, M. J. (Eds.). (1997). *Measuring patient changes in mood, anxiety, and personality disorders: Toward a core battery.* Washington, DC: American Psychological Association.

Tang, T. Z., & DeRubies, R. J. (1999a). Reconsidering rapid early response in cognitive-behavioral therapy for depression. *Clinical Psychology: Science and Practice, 6*(3), 283–288.

Tang, T. Z., & DeRubies, R. J. (1999b). Sudden gains and critical sessions in cognitive-behavioral therapy for depression. *Journal of Consulting and Clinical Psychology, 67(6),* 894–904.

Tingey, R. C., Lambert, M. L., Burlingame, G. M., & Hansen, N. B. (1996). Assessing clinical significance: Proposed extensions to the method. *Psychotherapy Research, 6,* 109–123.

Trull, T. J., Nietzel, M. T., & Main, A. (1988). The use of meta-analysis to assess the clinical significance of behavior therapy for agoraphobia. *Behavior Therapy, 19*(4), 527–538.

Umphress, V. J., Lambert, M. J., Smart, D. W., Barlow, S. H., & Clouse, G. (1997). Concurrent and construct validity of the Outcome Questionnaire. *Journal of Psychoeducational Assessment, 15,* 40–55.

Vermeersch, D. A., Lambert, M. J., & Burlingame, G. M. (2000). Outcome Questionnaire 45: Item sensitivity to change. *Journal of Personality Assessment, 74*(2), 242–261.

Vital signs (1998). Final report of the Ohio Mental Health Outcomes Task Force. Columbus, OH: Ohio Department of Mental Health.

Wampold, B. E. (2001). *The great psychotherapy debate: Models, methods, and findings.* Mahwah, NJ: Erlbaum.

Wampold, B. E., Mondin, G. W., Moody, M., Stich, F., Benson, K., & Ahn, H. (1997). A meta-analysis of outcome studies comparing bona fide psychotherapies: Empirically, "all must have prizes." *Psychological Bulletin, 122,* 203–215.

Ware, J. E. (1999). SF-36 Health Survey. In M. E. Maruish (Ed.), *The use of psychological testing for treatment planning and outcomes assessment* (2nd ed., pp. 1227–1246). Mahwah, NJ: Erlbaum.

Ware, J. E., Snow, K. K., Kosinski, M., & Gandek, B. (1993). *SF-36 Health Survey manual and interpretation guide.* Boston: New England Medical Center, The Health Institute.

Waskow, I. E., & Parloff, M. B. (1975). *Psychotherapy change measures.* Rockville, MD: National Institute of Mental Health.

Watkins, C. E. (1990). The testing the test section of the Journal of Counseling and Development: Historical, contemporary, and future perspectives. *Journal of Counseling and Development, 69,* 70–74.

Watkins, C. E. (Ed.). (1997). *Handbook of psychotherapy supervision.* New York: Wiley.

Weber, D. O. (1998). A field in its infancy: Measuring outcomes for children and adolescents. In K. J. Midgail (Ed.), *The behavioral outcomes & guidelines sourcebook* (pp. 201–205). Washington, DC: Faulkner and Gray's Healthcare Information Center.

Wechsler, D. (1974). *Manual for the Wechsler Intelligence Scale for Children—Revised.* San Antonio, TX: Psychological Corporation.

Wells, E. A., Hawkins, J. D., & Catalano, R. F. (1988). Choosing drug use measures for treatment outcome studies: I. The influence of measurement approach on treatment results. *International Journal of Drug Addiction, 23,* 851–873.

Wells, M. G., Burlingame, G. M., & Lambert, M. J. (1996). *Youth Outcome Questionnaire*

(YOQ). In M. E. Maruish (Ed.), *The use of psychological testing for treatment planning and outcomes assessment* (2nd ed. pp. 497–534). Mahwah, NJ: Erlbaum.

Wierzbicki, M., & Pekarik, G. (1993). A meta-analysis of psychotherapy dropout. *Professional Psychology: Research & Practice, 24,* 190–195.

Wiger, D. E., & Solberg, K. B. (2001). *Tracking mental health outcomes.* New York: Wiley.

Williams, S. L. (1985). On the nature and measurement of agoraphobia. *Progress in Behavior Modification, 19,* 109–144.

Wilson, G. T. (1999). Rapid response to cognitive behavior therapy. *Clinical Psychology: Science and Practice, 6,* 289–292.

Annotated Bibliography

Clement, P. W. (1999). *Outcome and incomes.* New York: Guilford.

Clement describes a method of evaluating outcomes in private practice that was honed by his own personal collection of outcome data over hundreds of clients. This unique method revolves around the use of a 10-point scale of functioning (SOF). Whether using tailored scales (instruments that are developed specifically for a client), symptom checklists, or standardized scales, the total scores are translated into the 10-point SOF score, and an effect size for the change from intake to end of treatment is calculated. Remaining chapters focus on developing a database to collect SOF effect sizes, methods of using the data, and multiple examples of forms and measures (including scale-to-SOF transformations). The book also comes with a CD that has many of the forms in electronic format.

Cone, J. D. (2001). *Evaluating outcomes: Empirical tools for effective practice.* Washington, DC: American Psychological Association.

This book covers a wide range of topics for improving practice from developing a personal vision statement for the practice to ethical issues in outcome evaluation. The book is written at a high level and includes a wealth of information. Chapters focus on the preparation for developing practice evaluation plans, along with detailed discussions of measurement tools, evaluation designs, analysis strategies, and advanced statistical and measurement topics. Examples of outcome evaluation are presented and ethical issues when evaluating outcome are considered. Finally, a chapter regarding the reporting of outcome to others (including the potential submission of such findings for publication) is included. Because of its comprehensiveness, this book makes an excellent reference and would be useful for graduate education. Some of the details, however, may be overkill for the private practitioner.

Cross, T. P., McDonald, E., & Lyons, H. (1997). *Evaluating the outcome of children's mental health services: A guide for the use of available child and family outcome measures* (2nd ed.). Boston: Judge Baker Children's Center.

This guide was written by the authors under contract with The Technical Assistance Center for the Evaluation of Children's Mental Health Systems at Judge Baker Children's Center. The book provides a brief introduction to the process of choosing measures, followed by the description of 32 different instruments divided into seven categories (behavioral problems, life functioning, family environment and behavior, etc.).

Hawkins, R. P., Mathews, J. R., & Hamdan, L. (1999). *Measuring behavioral health outcomes: A practical guide.* New York: Plenum.

This practical guide is focused on the assessment of outcomes for children and families. The book addresses the issue of outcome assessment from a more individualized behavioral approach to the

gathering of quantitative data. Chapters focus on selecting target behaviors to monitor and mea-
sure in various forms (e.g., frequency, latency, duration), using various rating scales and check-
lists, graphing or charting the data, engaging the family in the process of collecting observed data
in the home or other settings, interpreting the data, and troubleshooting problems that may arise
during the behavioral observations. In addition, several case examples are described.

Lyons, J. S., Howard, K. I., O'Mahoney, M. T., & Lish, J. D. (1997). *The measurement*
and management of clinical outcomes in mental health. New York: Wiley.

This book is perhaps the most sophisticated of the sources included in this annotated bibliogra-
phy; it is perhaps most appropriate for a managed-care organization that is interested in develop-
ing a practical, yet rigorous method of managing client outcomes in practice. Chapters cover the
measurement of clinical and utilization outcomes, including consumer satisfaction. Sophisticated
methods of managing outcome using patient-oriented research strategies are described, along with
methods of using the outcomes to improve quality. A chapter directed at helping organizations to
overcome barriers to implementing outcome assessment strategies is also included and is followed
by separate chapters that provide examples of outcome management in acute psychiatric care, out-
patient services, substance abuse services, services for children, and community-based services in
the system of care.

Lambert, M. J., Christensen, E. R., & DeJulio, S. S. (1983). *The assessment of psycho-*
therapy outcome. New York: Wiley.

This out-of-print edited book was the first to elaborate in a meaningful way regarding the issues
surrounding the selection of outcome measures for studies of psychotherapy research. The focus of
the book is a more academic approach to evaluating various measures that may be used in
psychotherapy outcome studies. Chapters cover a variety of instruments from clients', therapists',
observers', and others' point of view.

Maruish, M. E. (Ed.). (1999). *The use of psychological testing for treatment planning and out-*
comes assessment (2nd ed.). Mahwah, NJ: Erlbaum.

This is the second edition of an edited book that addresses the use of psychological tests for treat-
ment planning and outcome assessment. The initial chapters focus on a variety of general consid-
erations of the use of measures in practice, such as guidelines for selecting measures, designing out-
come management systems, and selecting statistical procedures. The remaining chapters each
describe one of 14 child and adolescent and 23 adult measures. These chapters are generally writ-
ten by the individual who developed the instrument.

Ogles, B. M., Lambert, M. J., & Masters, K. S. (1996). *Assessing outcome in clinical prac-*
tice. Boston: Allyn & Bacon.

This book's focus is directed toward the selection of outcome measures, with less information re-
garding the methods of implementing or using the data. Several frequently used measures are de-
scribed; chapters describe global measures, specific measures, individualized measures, and pro-
cess measures. A large appendix gives examples from the various measures, information

regarding where to obtain the measures, and basic psychometric data regarding each measure. In addition, data and figures useful for the calculation of clinical significance are provided.

Pfeiffer, S. I. (Ed.). (1996). Outcome assessment in residential treatment. *Residential Treatment for Children and Youth, 13*, 1–91.

This special journal issue focused on outcome assessment. Five articles address the historical issues involved in the assessment of outcome in general and in residential settings, the criteria for selecting measures of outcome, a comparison of various measures that are available, and the logistical, practical, and ethical issues that must be considered when implementing outcome assessment. Finally, a specific example of outcome assessment using the Devereux Scales of Mental Disorders is described.

Sederer, L. I. & Dickey, B. (Eds.). (1996). *Outcomes assessment in clinical practice.* Baltimore: Williams & Wilkins.

This edited book includes seven initial chapters that discuss the issues involved in integrating outcome assessment into practice. A variety of issues are discussed, including psychometrics, methodologies, uses of outcome data, and other conceptual issues. The next 16 chapters each describe one instrument that could be used in the assessment of outcomes. The instruments vary from specialized (e.g., eating disorder inventory) to general (e.g., SCL-90-R). The five remaining chapters discuss some of the potential issues of the future for outcome assessment, including practice networks, report cards, and practice guidelines.

Speer, D. C. (1998). *Mental health outcome evaluation.* San Diego, CA: Academic Press.

This book is focused on mental health evaluation and as such it is focused more on mental health service research with specific application to field settings. Chapters cover a variety of topics, including methods for determining whether change has occurred and determining what to measure; the book also describes potential problems that may interfere with data collection or interpretation, as well as practical suggestions for the implementation of outcome data collection.

United Way of America. (1996). *Measuring program outcomes: A practical approach.* Alexandria, VA: Author.

The United Way created a task force that drafted a practical guide for nonprofit organizations that were interested in planning and implementing outcome measurement for their programs. The manual gives excellent advice regarding the steps an organization may follow when preparing for a program evaluation that includes outcome measurement. They suggest that a work group be established within the organization to make the critical decisions around the outcome assessment implementation. They further suggest that this group actively participate from the earliest conversations to the examination of reports produced when the process is first operational. This type of group process may be realistic for many nonprofit community mental health agencies that are in the early stages of outcome assessment. For the private practitioner, however, the work group may consist of one person—the clinician. In addition, program evaluation within a nonprofit organization may be quite different from an independent practitioner's use of ongoing outcome assess-

ment with the individual client. Nevertheless, the manual provides a practical and well-written approach for implementing outcome evaluation for nonprofit organizations.

Waskow, I. E., & Parloff, M. B. (1975). *Psychotherapy change measures.* Rockville, MD: National Institute of Mental Health.

This manual summarizes the work of a NIMH conference that gathered experts in the field of psychotherapy research. The experts were pulled together to discuss the possible development of a core battery of outcome measures that could be used in studies of psychotherapy outcome. Individual chapters were written by each conference participant and each chapter ends with the author's recommendation for instruments to include in the core battery. In the closing chapters, a core battery is proposed and an imaginary interview is conducted with the psychotherapy researcher to describe how one might go about selecting instruments to include in the study. This book provides interesting historical reading, but many of the measures reviewed in the book and thought to be important 25 years ago are no longer relevant.

Wiger, D. E., & Solberg, K. B. (2001). *Tracking mental health outcomes.* New York: Wiley.

This practical book describes multiple methods of tracking outcomes that may be useful for the private practitioner. Chapters provide an overview and introduction to outcome assessment along with the need for assessment in current practice. In addition, individualized and normative approaches to outcome assessment are contrasted. Several potential methods of individualized (e.g., specific behaviors, change in diagnosis, use of the treatment plan or progress notes) or normative assessment (using examples from four common measures—OQ-45, SCL-90-R, BDI, and BASIS-32) are described in later chapters. Tips for selecting among measures and methods for collecting, analyzing, and reporting data are also included. Finally, this book comes with a disk that has several blank forms that can be used by the reader.

Index

About the Authors

Benjamin M. Ogles received his doctorate from Brigham Young University in 1990 after completing a predoctoral clinical internship at the Indiana University Medical School. He is currently the director of clinical training and an associate professor in the Department of Psychology at Ohio University. He has also been involved in clinical and consulting work for 19 years. He is the primary author of the Ohio Scales.

Michael J. Lambert received his doctorate from the University of Utah in 1971. He has been a practicing clinician for the past 30 years. He is currently a professor of psychology at Brigham Young University. He is the author of numerous articles and books on the effects of psychotherapy on client outcome and is the lead developer of the OQ-45.

Scott A. Fields is a doctoral candidate in the Ohio University Clinical Psychology program. He is currently completing his predoctoral internship at West Virginia University in Charleston. He has been involved in clinical work as a psychology assistant for the past 6 years and has coauthored several articles on two outcome assessment instruments: the Ohio Scales and the Abuse Disability Questionnaire.